Japan at the Brink

Japan at the Brink

KONOSUKE MATSUSHITA

translated by CHARLES S. TERRY

 KODANSHA INTERNATIONAL
Tokyo, New York & San Francisco

Distributors:
United States: *Kodansha International/USA Ltd., through Harper & Row, Publishers, Inc., 10 East 53 Street, New York, New York 10022.* South America: *Harper & Row, International Department.* Canada: *Fitzhenry & Whiteside Limited, 150 Lesmill Road, Don Mills, Ontario.* Mexico and Central America: *HARLA S. A. de C. V., Apartado 30–546, Mexico 4, D.F.* United Kingdom: *TABS, 7 Maiden Lane, London WC2.* Europe: *Boxerbooks Inc., Limmatstrasse 111, 8031 Zurich.* Australia and New Zealand: *Book Wise (Australia) Pty. Ltd., 104–8 Sussex Street, Sydney 2000.* Thailand: *Central Department Store Ltd., 306 Silom Road, Bangkok.* Hong Kong and Singapore: *Books for Asia Ltd., 30 Tat Chee Avenue, Kowloon; 65 Crescent Road, Singapore 15.* The Far East: *Japan Publications Trading Company, P.O. Box 5030, Tokyo International, Tokyo.*

Published by Kodansha International Ltd., 2–12–21 Otowa, Bunkyo-ku, Tokyo 112 and Kodansha International/USA Ltd., 10 East 53 Street, New York, New York 10022 and 44 Montgomery Street, San Francisco, California 94104. Copyright © 1975 by Kodansha Internationl Ltd. All rights reserved. Printed in Japan.

LCC 75–30180
ISBN 0–87011–269–4
First edition, 1976   *JBC 0036–785169–2361*

Contents

1939275

Part I: Grasping the Problem

An Unprecedented Situation

Recession

In the summer of 1973, the biggest of the postwar booms in Japan peaked out, and the first signs of recession set in. By the beginning of 1974, in the wake of the oil shock, some people were already warning that before long the economy would head straight down, that it would become more and more difficult to sell products, that interest costs would rapidly pile up, and that there would be a chain reaction of bankruptcies.

At the time, however, we were still suffering from the shortages of the previous year, and the most serious problem still seemed to be acquiring enough goods rather than disposing of them. As a result, throughout much of early 1974 there were many who took an optimistic view of the economy. Even after the annual "spring struggle" yielded the labor force an enormous wage increase, there were still people who argued that there was no reason to worry, because higher wages would lead to increased consumption. The summer bonuses, they said, would cause a great increase in consumer demand. In actual fact, there was a temporary increase in demand during the summer, but it was short-lived. To make matters worse, sales of so-called "summer goods" (air conditioners, refrigerators, and the like) were held down by a long rainy season and a relatively cool summer, and by fall it was apparent that a major recession was upon us. By the beginning of 1975, there were no longer many businessmen optimistic enough to predict an early recovery.

In March, 1975, the situation was considerably more serious than had seemed likely even in the previous fall. The credit crunch was continuing; sales were off badly; inventories were piling up; and companies were not only hiring fewer new workers, but in some instances soliciting volunteers for retirement among their current staffs. Both the number and the scale of bankruptcies were large and still on the rise.

Previous recessions had followed a classic pattern: a drop in sales would lead eventually to lower prices, and then sales would gradually pick up again. This time, however, it was different, because prices, far from decreasing, continued to climb at an alarming rate. The situation now, in the late spring of 1975, is worse than it has been since the country recovered from its wartime disaster.

And yet it seems to me that there are all too many people who do not realize just how grave our present situation has become. The widespread feeling seems to be, "Oh well, we've had depressions before, and we've always pulled through, so why worry and fret so much now?" Many businessmen seem to believe that though sales are off and money is tight in their particular businesses, there is no cause for general alarm. Of course, at times like these, particular businessmen and particular businesses find that they need to exercise special care, but I do not think the current recession is merely a matter of sales being off in a number of fields, or of credit continuing to be tight. Indeed, the situation in which Japan now finds itself goes beyond economics and involves much more important factors. The proof of this, I think, lies in the continued rise in prices despite the general stagnation of the economy, and in contrast to our expectations.

To state the case very simply, the Japanese government today is in a state of confusion, and as a result the people themselves are perplexed and troubled. Widespread unrest and uncertainty have become both the cause and the effect of our current dilemma, which is far more deeply rooted than a simple economic slump. If it were no more than that, it would be easy enough to loosen credit, put an end to tight money, and proceed on our merry way back to prosperity. The problem however, is too complicated for this shot-in-the-arm method, for it is clear that a monetary stimulus to the economy at this time would lead straight to another drastic rise in prices.

Poverty in the midst of plenty

The most serious recession we have experienced up until recently bottomed out in 1965, and there are many economists and businessmen who draw a comparison between that year and the present. Others consider that the current situation is more like the worldwide depression of the thirties or, despite the differences in causes, the difficult period that followed defeat in World War II. These two earlier experiences were certainly serious trials for the Japanese nation as a whole, but in some ways at least, the present predicament is even more frightening.

I do not mean to make light of the recession of 1965, for that was a bad year indeed. The nation's top producer of special steel collapsed, and one of the largest securities firms in the country would have had to declare bankruptcy if it had not been bailed out with an extraordinary loan from the Bank of Japan. Countless smaller businesses went under.

Still, that recession concerned primarily the business community. Several years of unprecedented prosperity had led to managerial laxness and excess competition, and as soon as the business cycle entered a downturn, these evils not only became apparent, but also contributed to making the depression worse than it might otherwise have been. And yet, particular industries and the economic community as a whole were able to ride it out through a combination of self-criticism and hard work. The lessons learned at that time enabled the Japanese economy to grow at a rapid pace in later years, and for a time the level of exports rose so high that for the first time in our lives we were troubled by a superfluity of foreign currency.

The point we must appreciate today is that the present recession is different in nature from earlier ones, and it cannot be cured by the efforts of the business community alone. Obviously, individual businesses and the economic community as a whole will have to adjust to new conditions and to put up an energetic struggle against the problems that exist. In my opinion, however, we will not accomplish what needs to be accomplished unless the economic effort is accompanied by important political reforms and by a general re-awakening of the spirit.

We were in a piteous state just after the war, for we lacked not only industrial materials, but even food. We have talked of shortages in the months since the oil crisis, but today the shortages are not absolute, as they were then. On the contrary, we are surrounded by an abundance of material things.

Still, we had something in those postwar years that we seem to lack now, namely the national will, even in the midst of poverty and want, to pull out of our slump, to produce goods, to rebuild our economy, and to improve our standard of living. Nearly every Japanese shared this determination, whether he said anything about it or not, and it became the foundation upon which a new and flourishing economy was built. We encountered many hurdles along the way, but our unified will was strong enough for us to overcome them. The result was that even after a shattering military defeat, along with all the concomitant unrest and confusion, we were able to carry out an economic expansion that became a source of amazement to the rest of the world.

Today we have lots of possessions, and we enjoy one of the highest standards of living in the world. There is plenty of food, for a price, and jobs are available for those who want to work (or at least at the time of writing, unemployment has not become a serious problem). Yet when it comes to the question of whether we still have the unity of spirit we once had, the answer must be in the negative. Unity of purpose is to be found neither among our politicians nor in our everyday dealings with one another. The people are badly divided, and everyone pursues his own ends, without thought for his neighbor or the nation as a whole. We have grown suspicious of each other; we attack each other bitterly. After the war, we were all in the depths of poverty, but we knew quite clearly what had to be done. Now, we enjoy a degree of affluence, but we are puzzled as to what we should do and how we should live. In many ways this bewilderment is more distressing, more difficult to bear, than the discomforts of the early postwar period.

In the early thirties, too, we were engulfed by the

waves of worldwide depression, and at a time when our economy was much smaller and weaker than it is today. Still, in those days, we had a government that knew what it was doing, and we managed to put the depression behind us. Whether our present government can furnish similar leadership remains to be seen.

Another Italy?

During the last year, reports from abroad have indicated that Italy is on the verge of national bankruptcy. If we may believe what we read, the same Italy that carried out an economic miracle in the 1960's is now confronted not only with a staggering outflow of foreign currency, but with galloping domestic inflation and an alarming rise in unemployment. One newspaper quoted a former financial minister as saying that "the situation is completely out of control, and we are reduced to grasping at straws." It would appear that without massive aid from other countries, the whole nation would have gone under before now.

Britain, too, is suffering from the same "trilemma" of rising prices, increased unemployment, and serious deficits in the foreign currency account. When the Labour Party won in the last general elections, newspaper accounts indicated that there was far less rejoicing among Labour leaders over the victory than there was concern for the difficulties lying ahead. I cannot refrain from asking myself today what happened to the great British Empire that once dominated the oceans.

We of Japan, however, must not lull ourselves into the notion that the problems confronting England and Italy have nothing to do with us. There are, of course, certain differences between Japan on the one hand and Italy and England on the other. But what has happened in Italy and England could very easily happen in Japan as it is now, and certainly will happen if Japan continues on its present course. People are prone to dismiss as pure science fiction the recent *Submergence of Japan*, which was successful both as a novel and as a movie. But in fact Japan today is on the verge of capsizing, politically, economically, and spiritually. Nor is there any easy remedy for the sickness that prevails.

First and foremost, we must all recognize just how serious the present situation is. Then we must consider together what we can and must do to avoid national collapse. In the following pages, I have outlined the dangers as I see them and offered a number of suggestions whereby I think we could, all working together, avoid the catastrophe that now seems imminent.

Japan at the Brink of Collapse

Inflation and the oil crisis

Most people consider inflation to be the most important of the various economic problems confronting Japanese society today, and they are right. A runaway rise in prices that started with the oil crisis had by the end of 1974 proceeded so far as to impose a very real threat to the national livelihood, exerting at the same time a baleful influence on economic activity throughout the country. Today, there is some hope that the rise in prices for the current year can be held below the ten percent level, but ten percent is by no means a small increase, and inflation remains a tremendous burden on the people as a whole. For the housewife, there is the daily dilemma of how to balance the household budget amid ever-increasing prices; for the industrialist there is the constant problem of finding ways to absorb rising costs resulting not only from higher wages but from the soaring cost of raw materials.

Inflation in Japan today, I think, presents two

major aspects. One is basic inflation, by which I mean a steady trend toward higher and higher prices regardless of outside factors. This is caused, directly or indirectly, by waste, loss, or inefficiency in our national way of life, and in this I include all our various activities, whether political, economic, social, or otherwise. The simple fact is that over a good number of years, wasteful or inefficient living has gradually pushed up the price we must pay for what we receive.

The other aspect of current inflation is directly connected with the vastly increased price of oil. Last year, the two phases of inflation, namely the constant, basic trend and the sudden, extraordinary spurt resulting from the oil crisis, combined to produce a wild spiral of price increases.

When the oil-producing nations of the Middle East raised the price of crude petroleum from $2.50 to $10, they were in effect quadrupling the cost of much of the world's industrial energy, as well as one of the world's most important raw materials. The effect was bound to be felt in all countries, and particularly in Japan, where for at least two decades the relatively low cost of oil had led to the neglect of other possible sources of energy, such as coal or hydroelectric power. If the threat to Japan was greater than to many other nations, it was nevertheless true that the increase in the price of oil created inflationary pressures throughout the world, whether in the fully industrialized countries or in the developing nations. The effects were particularly serious in Italy and England, but they were felt even in West Germany, despite that country's justly deserved reputation for being the industrial nation with the most solid economic structure and the most stable prices. In Brazil, which had succeeded after years of effort in bringing under control its once disastrous rate of inflation, the increase in the price of oil sparked another large rise in prices.

There is no doubt but that a general rise in prices after the fourfold increase in the price of oil was inevitable. If the increase in the cost of oil had been thirty percent, or even fifty percent, it might conceivably have been possible for certain nations to absorb this by taking steps to increase their industrial productivity, but no amount of effort would have enabled them to offset the rise that was actually exacted. This was an unprecedented challenge to economies everywhere, and one that defied economic common sense.

Even so, if the Japanese inflation had been a matter of an increase in the price of oil alone, after other prices had been adjusted to an appropriate new level, it should have been possible to achieve price stability. Indeed, I think it actually might have been possible to stabilize prices if we had united, as a nation and as a people, in deciding upon and implementing strong anti-inflationary measures. But here is where we failed, for the measures adopted were either inadequate or inappropriate, and the result was inflation—on a scale far exceeding that which could have been justified by the oil crisis alone. In my opinion, it is still not too late to ask ourselves what we did wrong, and why we were unable, when the time came, to adopt expedient and effective methods of dealing with the problem.

No worldwide anti-monopoly law

At the time of the oil crisis, what would have happened if there had existed a worldwide anti-monopoly law and a worldwide fair trade commission to implement it? The collective action of the oil-producing countries in quadrupling prices would no doubt have infringed upon the provisions of this law, and the worldwide fair trade commission would have taken the price increase under immediate consideration. The commission would probably have tried to prohibit the oil-producing nations from raising the price of oil at all and, failing that, would have pointed out to them the economic chaos that would result from such an increase and advised them to proceed more gradually. In any case, the commission would certainly have reasoned with the producing nations and urged them to adopt less drastic measures.

Unfortunately, of course, there is neither a worldwide anti-monopoly law now, nor a worldwide fair trade commission. We have, to be sure, the United Nations, but it does not engage in activities of this sort. My question, however, is: why didn't Japan at least attempt to follow the course that a worldwide fair trade commission would have adopted? In other words, why didn't Japan unilaterally try to reason with the oil-producing nations? I myself think that the Japanese government should have done just this and, while negotiating with the producing countries, should have worked to put its policy across to the Japanese people, whose unified support it would have needed to see its policy through.

The government approach toward the oil-producing nations ought to have run more or less as follows: "If you raise the price of oil four times all at once, you will not only create basic problems affecting the livelihood of the people of Japan, but you will also make it more difficult for Japan to supply yourselves and other developing countries with the goods made from petroleum or manufactured with the energy derived from it. The damage will affect not only Japan, but the countries importing from Japan, and eventually it will extend to the whole world. If you consider that the price of oil is too low, then by all means raise it, but instead of quadrupling it right now, carry out your price increase gradually over a period of, say, five years, which will make it possible for us somehow to absorb the difference. All we ask is that you give us time."

A proposal outlining such a plea should have been adopted by the National Diet on a nonpartisan basis, and the argument should have been presented to the oil countries by a special ambassador, acting on behalf of the Japanese people as a whole.

Considering the state of affairs at the time of the oil crisis, I am not at all sure that the oil-producing countries would have agreed unconditionally, or at all, to a Japanese proposal of this sort, but they might have if they had known if was supported by the Japanese people in its entirety. In any event, if the government had followed this procedure, the people would have understood what the government was attempting to do, and at a later stage it would have been easier for the government to appeal to the national conscience for aid in controlling inflation. The government could have said to the people, in effect, "Now, we have done what we could to prevent this tremendous increase in the price of oil, and we have failed, through no fault of our own. In the coming months, it is essential that we all remain calm and approach the problem sensibly. The increase in the price of oil is of necessity going to cause a general rise in prices, but if we all keep our heads, this increase need not go beyond a certain definite point. The government will take such measures as are necessary to prevent inflation from exceeding this limit, and we ask that you, too, keep your wits about you and refrain from trying to make a killing by using the oil-price increase as an excuse for otherwise unjustified price increases. If you start raising prices willy-nilly, the result will be a staggering blow to the national economy, and eventually to you yourselves."

I think that such an appeal might well have been appreciated and heeded by the Japanese people as a whole, and if this had actually happened, the crisis brought on by the oil shock, serious though it was, would not have been insuperable. In fact, the effect might have been the creation of sufficient harmony among the people to make the transition to higher price levels a smooth and well-coordinated operation.

What happened, however, was that far from creating a policy supported by a national consensus, the government adopted no policy at all. As a result, the people did not know how to react, and individuals, as well as enterprises, went from right to left and back again confronting the oil crisis as best they could. In some instances they took advantage of it to make huge profits on the products they were selling. This created a mountain of bitter distrust in the body politic, and for a time everybody was blaming everybody else for the nation's difficulties. In effect, for lack of a clear policy, and for lack of any assurance that the price rises brought on by the oil crisis would be brought under control at some definite level, the inflationary pressure resulting from the oil-price increase was magnified beyond all need, and many prices having no connection whatever with oil were raised drastically. All this came on top of the inflationary trend already in existence, and as of this writing we have not yet succeeded in bringing spiraling prices under satisfactory control.

The most expensive city in the world

It is no exaggeration to say that prices in Japan today are higher than anywhere else in the world. According to a recent television survey, the results of a study by a team of foreign experts indicate that Tokyo is now the world's most expensive city. Furthermore, Osaka is the second most expensive, and Yokohama the third. Paris, notorious in the West for its outrageous prices, ran a poor fourth, and New York was far behind in eleventh position.

Until only a few years ago, New York was regarded as the world's greatest city, and for good reason, since it is the most populous and richest city in the world's richest country. People have generally considered, too, that since the residents of New York commanded a higher income than people anywhere else, it was only to be expected that prices in that city would be the highest in the world. In the past, countless Japanese visitors have come away with the impression that New York was the highest-priced place on earth, but now we find it ranking far lower than Tokyo and other large Japanese cities in the race for this dubious distinction. From this it is not hard to guess that prices throughout Japan are higher than anywhere else.

A general increase in prices constitutes a threat to our daily lives, and a variety of recent surveys have shown that the people of Japan are more worried about inflation than about anything else. The same surveys naturally show that what the people want most from the government is an effective program for price stabilization.

The trouble with inflation is that it affects everybody and everything. I happen to be the chairman of the board of directors of a certain foundation, and I am appalled at the effect of the recent inflation on this organization's finances. Like other foundations, it works on a budget and tries to handle its affairs in such a way that annual expenditures will be approximately equal to annual income. When, in November, 1973, the budget for 1974 was drawn up, income and outgo alike were calculated at approximately ¥300,000,000 (about $1,000,000). As it turned out in 1974, income indeed amounted to about this figure, but because of increased expenses for wages and other costs, the foundation went into the red by about ¥70,000,000.

This foundation could be taken as typical of the situation that prevails throughout Japan today. With a few exceptions, all public organizations and associations are experiencing similar trouble with their budgets: expenses continue to rise at a dizzying rate, while income remains fixed. This is true, also, of local governments in Japan, both at the metropolitan level and at the prefectural level. One reads constantly in the newspapers about local governments in such an economic bind that they have had to curtail new employment, or postpone construction of schools, or drop plans for other public facilities. Stoppage of work on public projects because of the high cost of building materials and construction labor has become almost a daily occurrence.

The same phenomenon is arising, if it has not already arisen, at the national level. In 1974, an increase in revenues due to higher wage levels and a higher corporate tax rate made it possible for the government, on the surface at least, to meet its obligations, but there is every prospect that the government will be operating in the red in 1975. Recent newspaper reports indicate that despite the expected increase in national revenues, the Minister of Finance believes that rising expenses will make it impossible to carry out any significant reduction in taxes. If taxes are not reduced as revenues increase, then what we actually have is a rise in taxes, and if the government feels constrained to raise the level of taxation in this fashion, it stands to reason that the government is operating at a deficit.*

Management and inflation

Business also suffers greatly from inflation, despite the belief of many that inflation brings profits to businessmen at the expense of ordinary people. It is true, I think, that certain businesses have in the past profited from

*In the few months since this was written, it has become evident that revenues for 1975 will be far less than predicted, and that the government is in fact confronted with a huge deficit.

inflationary trends. This, however, is no longer the case to any appreciable extent, because businesses themselves are great buyers and consumers of goods. A general increase in prices creates a distinct burden on businessmen, who must purchase the commodities and products required to keep their operations going. Theoretically, it might be possible to pass on the rising cost of operation to the consumer, but in a competitive economy such as our own, this is often unfeasible. In particular, during a recession such as the one we are going through now, it is difficult to sell anything to begin with, and price increases are frequently completely out of the question. Today, many Japanese businessmen are caught in a bind between rising production costs and selling prices that cannot be raised.

True, the businessman enjoys greater freedom of action than do those in charge of foundations, local governments, or the national government. If the businessman is clever, for example, he may devise means of raising productivity or expanding sales or achieving significant savings, whereas the people in charge of foundations and governments are typically without such alternatives. Today, most businessmen are managing through their own enterprise to show a certain amount of profit. But the ratio of profit is gradually declining, and if things keep up as they are now, the number of businesses operating in the red is bound to increase.

There is also an international aspect to rising costs, for Japan cannot afford to price its products out of the going world market. We have already seen that consumer prices are higher in Japan than anywhere else, and this goes double for land prices, which constitute one of the foundations on which all economic activity rests. In past decades, Japanese wage levels were far lower than in the more advanced industrial nations; but now, if bonuses and severance pay and a number of worker benefits peculiar to Japan are included in the calculation, the average hourly wage in this country is higher than in Europe. Indeed, it may well be that as a result of the tremendous wage hikes of 1974, the Japanese wage level in certain areas will be as high as or higher than that in the United States, and the upward trend continues.

Land is high. Wages are high. Prices are high. And all this in a country which, for lack of its own natural resources, must rely upon imports to keep its industrial machine operating. In face of the rising price of our products, will we in the end be able to compete in the international market and continue to expand our exports as needed? This may not be impossible, but it is obviously not going to be easy either.

If exports ceased?

Until now, Japan has followed a policy of promoting

exports, and this has served as a great motivating power in the rapid expansion of our economy. Japan's ability to increase its exports has, of course, been due in part to the high quality of Japanese products, but we must not forget that certain other factors have worked to Japan's advantage. For one thing, until recently, both wages and prices were lower in Japan than in Europe and America. For another, there have been no important restrictions on the import of raw materials from abroad, and since Japan is surrounded by ocean, it has been possible to ship these materials in at relatively low marine freight rates. Japanese products, therefore, have been able to compete successfully in world markets not only because of their quality, but because their price has been low.

In the past few years, however, the competitive advantage has begun rapidly to disappear. Domestic wages and prices have gone up enormously, and as can be seen from the case of oil alone, our supply of the necessary raw materials has grown more and more tenuous. Even when materials are available, they cost much more than they used to.

Under the circumstances, the cost of Japanese products is increasing rapidly. Even though the excellence of many Japanese products is recognized in foreign countries, this is only one small factor in the highly competitive international market. It is not easy to stay alive in international trade without being able to offer a cost advantage. Unless we can develop a constant stream of new and superlative products, Japan will certainly face difficult times in the export market before too long.

All this has a serious bearing on the national livelihood. It is bad enough when individual enterprises cease to be able to sell their products, but a general stagnation of the whole country's exports would affect far more than a few lines of business. Our whole economy is dependent upon the foreign currency that exports bring in, even though these exports amount to only a tenth or so of our gross national product. Since we are so severely lacking in natural resources of our own, we must import a wide variety of goods just to satisfy our own needs and keep our economy going. Today, we are dependent on foreign countries not only for natural resources used in manufacture, but even for much of the food we eat. We produce ourselves only about seventy percent of the agricultural and dairy end products that go into our mouths, and if one takes into consideration the imported feed and fertilizer used by Japanese farmers, as well as the oil needed to run agricultural machinery, our degree of self-sufficiency in the food area may well be less than fifty percent. At least, some critics think so.

In short, in order to sustain the lives of our 110,000,000 people, we buy a huge quantity of food and natural products from abroad. We are able to do this not only because the foreign countries are willing to sell to us, but because we earn enough foreign currency from our exports to make the necessary payments. Our customary procedure is to import raw materials, process them in various ways, and sell our products at a profit. If it becomes difficult for us to export, it will also become difficult to obtain foreign currency with which to buy the raw materials and food that we need. The result would be a threat not only to our overall economic activity, but to our very lives; without imports of foreign food, many Japanese would go hungry, or perhaps even starve. Such is the fate that is bearing down on us at this very moment.

Paying the piper

High prices in the midst of inflation, the whole country operating in the red, a threatened foreign-currency crisis because of the difficulty of exporting our products—these symptoms indicate that Japan is now well along the same path as Italy and England. We have experienced depressions before, and we know the hardships involved. But in the past, after a season of recession, prices would decrease, or at least level off. As a result, our products would become more competitive in the international market, and our exports would increase, thus providing an impetus for a return to prosperity in the domestic economy. We have been taught that this is in accordance with good economic theory, and our experience in the past has led most of us to believe that this is simply the way things work.

But now the situation is different. We are undeniably in a recession, and prices, far from declining, continue to rise. Sales remain very sluggish, and it is becoming increasingly difficult to export our products. We are facing a dilemma we have not previously encountered.

As mentioned earlier, standard procedure for stimulating sales would be to loosen credit, and there are many businessmen today who are clamoring for easy money. This time, however, if the credit reins are relaxed without extreme caution, it is a foregone conclusion that prices will rise still higher. Higher prices would create greater buyer resistance, and this would make it still harder to sell products in the domestic market. Here again it is difficult to go either forward or backward.

The ultimate reason for our impasse is simply that our problems do not result from economic causes alone. There is no doubt that the great increase in the price of oil and other commodities imported from abroad has been an important influencing factor, but if this were the only problem, I feel sure we could devise economic ways to cope with it. The more serious cause is our basic chronic inflation, which, as I have stated earlier, results from wastefulness and inefficiency in our whole way of life. It is not so much that we are living beyond our means as that we are dissipating the resources we possess.

During the postwar years, little by little, almost

imperceptibly, an element of wastefulness and inefficiency crept into our political framework, our educational system, and our attitudes toward life in general. Gradually, this element grew larger and larger, but instead of recognizing it and attempting to eliminate it, we tended to dismiss it as unimportant or peripheral. Growing steadily more serious over the years, it had the effect of pushing up prices bit by bit until we arrived at the point where a shock from without nearly sent us over the brink.

If I may be allowed to liken our condition to an illness, what we are suffering from is not a cold in the head or a fever or a stomachache arising from something we ate. It is a serious internal disorder of the sort that comes from years of neglecting one's health. It cannot be remedied by a dose or two of a patent medicine. It requires major surgery, accompanied by a basic change in our psychology. The operation will be painful, but it is the only solution. We brought the illness on ourselves through our own neglect, and we must bear the consequences.

It will be necessary for everyone to share the pain of the operation. For thirty years we have ignored what should not have been ignored, and failed to consider what should have been considered. We are now reaping the seeds we sowed. And make no mistake: we are all in this together. This is no time for everybody to be running around blaming everybody else for our predicament, nor can we escape our individual respon sibility. The most important question is whether we are now psychologically able to face up to our obligations and share the burden of settling them.

Distrust, Discontent, Dissatisfaction

1939275

A nation of squabblers

What we need today in order to overcome the current crisis is, first and foremost, the ability to work together as a people. Unless we acquire, or rather recover, that ability, I think that our country is on the road to ruin. Unfortunately, Japan today is characterized by disaccord: the people are divided, and everyone is going his separate way. When something bad happens, everybody blames and criticizes somebody else. We are vindictive toward each other, and we are constantly quarreling and fighting. We have become a nation of squabblers, dissipating our energies on nonproductive strife.

This situation was brought into clear focus by the oil crisis. The fact was that no one in Japan, not one single person, had the slightest responsibility for the fourfold increase in the price of oil. This was something that the oil-producing countries got together about and decided upon by themselves. There was nothing that the

Japan Fair Trade Commission could do about it, no way in which the Japanese Anti-Monopoly Law could have been invoked against it. Any plea or any request for concessions that we might have issued would have had to be addressed not to other Japanese like ourselves, but to the oil-producing nations. As I have said before, I think the proper approach would have been for the Japanese nation as a whole to request that the oil producers make certain modifications to avoid jeopardizing our national livelihood. If this had not worked, however, we would have had to resolve to roll up our sleeves and do what we could for ourselves, as we might in the case of a natural disaster such as a large earthquake or a typhoon.

When a natural disaster occurs, everybody is the victim, and we are all able somehow not only to sympathize and commiserate with our fellows, but to cooperate in helping each other out. In the case of the oil crisis, however, our reaction was almost the direct opposite. There being no clear-cut national policy to deal with the situation, we scurried about in numerous different directions, everyone thinking of nothing but protecting his own position. There was a wild scramble to buy up available goods, often goods not actually needed. Certain businessmen took advantage of this situation and held their products back until they could sell them at outrageous prices. Others, hardly less culpable, raised prices simply because everybody else was doing it. The conduct of these entrepreneurs was a violation of business ethics, as well as a repudiation of social responsibility, and the businessmen or companies involved contributed materially to making a bad situation much worse. They were, it is gratifying to report, roundly criticized, and they deserved it. Let us hope that the fire they came under for a time has impressed them with the error of their ways.

At the same time, if we focus on the issue of profiteers, there is a danger that we will lose sight of the larger problems and thereby introduce new elements of confusion. It is all right to expose profiteers, all right to punish them, all right to take measures to prevent similar profiteering in the future. But if we spend all our time and energy on this, rather than recognizing the more basic causes of profiteering, we are being wasteful. In the long run, we will do ourselves no service by allowing the knowledge that a number of businesses have been unethical to lead us to the conclusion that all business is bad, for in the first place this is not true, and in the second place it makes for still more wasteful distrust and disunity.

The oil-producing countries, for their part, are using the vast profits that they derive from the price increase to stimulate their domestic economic development and provide better welfare benefits for their people. There is nothing wrong with this, and it is certainly no reason why we, as the victims of the situation, should waste our time attacking each other and adding salt to our own wounds. It is as though a farmer upstream had polluted a river, and the farmers downstream were fighting among themselves over which of them was the guilty party. We would do better to bury our differences and increase our efficiency.

Distrust is inflationary

The number of court cases in Japan has increased tremendously over the past few years. Because of this, many new judges have been appointed, but the number of judges has not kept pace with the demand. I do not pretend to have studied this matter, and I have no sure way of knowing why there is so much more litigation than there used to be, but I strongly suspect that it is caused by the same deep-rooted distrust that underlay the divisive Japanese reaction to the oil crisis. In the past, the people of Japan were more prone than either Europeans or Americans to talk over their differences with each other and attempt to arrive at an amicable settlement. People appealed to the courts for decisions only in the most difficult cases. Indeed, going to court was considered, if not downright shameful, at least bad form, and people tended to avoid it no matter how just their claims. It was generally considered that two decent people ought to be able, by talking things over, to come to some sort of compromise.

To reach a settlement through negotiation, however, presupposes that the parties to a dispute trust each other to some extent. If there is no mutual trust whatever, there is no way to resolve things in a reasonable fashion, and it becomes necessary to appeal to a court for a black-and-white decision.

We see examples of distrust all around us. It is rampant, for example, in our universities. As centers of higher learning, the universities might be expected also to be centers of exemplary conduct; but instead we see college students of different political persuasions beating each other, even killing each other, with clubs and metal bars. From time to time, professors are subjected to kangaroo courts, university presidents confined to their offices, or important research facilities shut down for a matter of months or years. There is bitter suspicion between students and teachers, as well as among various student factions.

One sees a similar though less extreme lack of mutual confidence between parents and children, between laborers and employers, between producers and consumers, between political parties of different shades, and between the government and the people, which is causing tremendous loss to the nation, particularly in the increasingly numerous instances in which it blocks all efforts at compromise or positive action of any sort.

In a household where distrust reigns, there is apt to be constant bickering and antagonism between husband and wife or between parents and children. The lack of peace and happiness at home becomes a constant psychological burden on all concerned, and the effects are immediately visible in the outside performance of the household members. Typically, the father is unable to put himself fully into his work, and the children neglect their studies or run away or become involved in some form of delinquency. From the objective viewpoint, the father will fail to produce as much as he might produce, and the children will fall behind their classes or become, in one way or another, a burden on society. In effect, mutual distrust in the family becomes a negative factor materially as well as psychologically.

Within any given business enterprise, a lack of trust between managers and employees will inevitably result in lower efficiency. It proved enormously difficult and time-consuming to revamp the fading coal industry in Japan, for example, because extreme suspicion between the labor union and management made dialogue impossible. Similarly, if there is no basic element of trust among the political parties in the National Diet, it is impossible to hope for smooth deliberations in which differences of opinion are ironed out, and the business of running the nation attended to systematically and constructively.* Today, for lack of trust, Diet discussions tend to disintegrate into stubborn wrangling, if not into fistfights, and important legislation is

*As this book was being prepared for press, the Diet ended an especially stormy forty-day extended session, during which most of its time was spent in dilatory political maneuvering, and most of the key bills under consideration ended up being shelved.

held up interminably. Often the regular Diet sessions have to be extended, and even so, they frequently end up accomplishing little.

Directly or indirectly, inefficiency caused by widespread distrust is one of the main factors that have caused prices to rise as high as they have. In a broad sense, we must number among the causes of inflation all the instances of strife I have cited: the destruction that has resulted from the student struggle, the increase in the number of court cases and the concomitant increase in the nation's expenditure for courts, the reduction of efficiency that comes from bad labor-management relations, and the political inaction caused by endless bickering among political parties.

I have distinguished earlier between the temporary inflationary pressure that arose from the increase in oil prices and the more important inflationary pressure resulting from wastefulness and inefficiency. We tend to think of inefficiency more or less in terms of purely economic factors—inadequate machinery, below-capacity operation, faulty use of personnel, slack financial management, and so on—but none of these factors, I think, is either as important or as fundamental as the atmosphere of suspicion to be found at all levels of society. This is the most damaging factor I can think of in our national life, and especially because most people fail to connect it with the material waste and non-productivity of which it is the root cause.

What we must all do now is reflect on the seeds of

distrust that lurk in many of our national activities and try somehow to avoid actions which make our situation worse. We must not be too quick to condemn others on the strength of their having done something not to our liking. If we are to solve our present dilemma, we must adopt a more generous and tolerant attitude toward each other, and attempt by doing so to eliminate the causes of suspicion. I cannot pinpoint when or where we lost our sense of mutuality, but I see that its recovery is basic to our future survival.

Lack of self-reliance

Another important reason for the increasing social unrest in Japan is the attitude of dependence displayed by so many Japanese today. We rely entirely too much on others for assistance; we seem to have the unconscious belief that if things go wrong, someone will come to our rescue. Looked at from a different angle, this means that as individuals and as a people, we lack the self-reliance and spirit of independence needed to do things on our own.

In one sense, our lack of self-reliance can be traced back to the process whereby Japan was reconstructed after the war. Defeat left us with nothing. Starting from there, we pulled ourselves together and set about reviving and rebuilding the nation. The work and energy that we devoted to this task are by no means to be underestimated. Despite countless difficulties, we not only rebuilt what we had before, but went on to achieve a degree of economic growth and sophistication that has evoked the world's admiration. This is, I think, an achievement of which many Japanese are proud, and justly so.

We all too often forget, however, that we did not achieve our economic miracle entirely on our own. From the beginning America and several other advanced nations lent a helping hand, and it would be fitting to say that their assistance at the right time was what made the recovery of Japan possible.

Immediately after the war, for example, we suffered from a terrible food shortage. If we had not been both careful and lucky, it is possible that many, many people would have starved. Indeed, one scrupulous Japanese judge did die of starvation because he refused to eat anything but his legal rations. In those terrible times, however, the United States came to our rescue with aid in the form of foodstuffs; our diet remained meager, but at least disaster was averted.

Similar considerations apply to our economic recovery and continued growth. Japanese industry can claim much credit for carrying out the expansion that has allowed us in only thirty years to achieve the second largest gross national product among the free nations. But it is also true that this growth was made possible by a technological revolution in which we drew heavily on the scientific achievements of other countries. We arrived at our present ability to produce and supply superior products by adopting the most modern techniques and facilities available, almost none of which was originally developed in Japan. Postwar Japanese industry was founded and expanded on methods first invented in America and the more advanced countries of Europe.

We did not by any means receive these technical improvements gratis. All the patents and know-how we have imported were necessarily paid for. Still, we must not forget that the more advanced countries could, had they wanted to, have refused to let us use their methods even for money, for we were after all potential rivals. Still, for the most part, these countries made their scientific and technical achievements available to us. If they had not, and if all the scientific techniques we adopted had had to be developed independently in Japan, the cost might well have been several tens of times the amount paid out in royalties and patent fees, and there is no telling how long the necessary research would have required. Many methods now in standard use might still be on the drawing boards. Japan is immensely indebted for the technical discoveries it has imported to date.

Something similar could be said with respect to natural resources. In very recent years, owing to the depletion of the world's resources, it has become difficult to acquire all the materials we need, but during most of the postwar period, the countries that possessed these materials were willing to sell them to us in any quantity that our industries desired.

In short, Japan's postwar development has been carried out to a considerable degree with the aid and goodwill of foreign countries. There are, of course, quite a few countries which despite much aid from abroad during the same period have proved unable to put it to effective use, and it is certainly to Japan's credit that the aid, technical know-how, and raw materials received from foreign countries have been employed to such great advantage. The Japanese people, I believe, also deserve praise for their willingness to work.

I wonder, however, if we have not become too complacent in our dependence on others. We seem to have convinced ourselves that so long as we can pay the money, foreign countries will be delighted to furnish us with technical improvements and raw materials. As a result, we have neglected, and are neglecting, to prepare ourselves either materially or spiritually for a situation in which we might not be able to purchase that which we need. Our shock at finding that our easy dependence on foreign countries was not necessarily realistic added greatly to the confusion that followed the oil crisis.

Weak government

The tendency to rely on others has become widespread

not only in our foreign relations, but even within Japan. A prime example is the fashion in which Japanese business concerns depend so heavily on loans for their operating capital.

Using data from *Fortune* magazine, I recently compared the ten largest Japanese and the ten largest American corporations with respect to their degree of reliance on their own capital. Among the American companies, the average percentage was 54.6%, but among the Japanese firms, it was no more than 18.5%. In other words, large American companies cover more than half of their needs with their own capital, whereas large Japanese firms rely on bank loans for more than eighty percent of their requirements. One can only conclude from this that Japanese business is from the financial viewpoint much more fragile than American business.

Just after the war, of course, it was all but inevitable that Japanese business would have to rely largely on loans, for we had all lost nearly everything, and it was necessary to start all over again. Nobody had the capital needed to revive the economy or provide the products needed by the people, and the only way to put the economy back on its feet was for us to lend each other the little we had. It worked, and the economy grew, and everybody was exceedingly happy. Consequently, it would be difficult from the pragmatic viewpoint to fault the high-debt management that business resorted to in those days. Now, however, we have long since passed the stage at which companies should have ceased relying on bank loans and begun operating on their own money. This is the classical mode of entrepreneurial operation, and it is the proper one in a capitalistic system. What has happened, however, is that we have allowed an emergency measure, necessitated by the postwar shortage of capital, to become normal procedure. Indeed, the whole system of financing through loans has been vastly expanded, with the result that the economy, while having displayed a tremendous growth rate, nevertheless retains an element of basic financial shakiness. Furthermore this structural flaw extends to the psychological level, for Japanese business leaders today, instead of financing their own undertakings, still prefer the easier method of relying on the banks for investment capital.

During the same postwar period, the people as a whole developed the habit of making constant demands of one sort or another on the government, on the political parties, or on local administrative authorities. In particular, in the past few years there has been an increasing clamor for greater welfare benefits, even for the establishment of a welfare state. In response to these pressures, the government and the politicians have made all sorts of promises that they may or may not be able to fulfill.

To provide improved welfare benefits for the people is an excellent thing, and one which in a fundamental sense needs to be encouraged. The question is, who is to pay for these benefits? In form, at least, the government and the political parties and the local administrations dole out the money, but this money does not, after all, come ultimately from them. They have neither a money tree nor a magic wand. Whatever other financial ramifications are involved, welfare benefits are ultimately paid for with taxes, which are the product of the people's hard work.

It is always pleasant to hear that the government or the political parties are going to do this, that, or the other for us, but the truth of the matter is that they themselves are not the source of the power to deliver. They are entirely reliant on the fact that the people, business included, work very hard and turn over in taxes roughly half the fruits of their labor. And we in Japan act as if we have forgotten this fact.

For the people to make demands on the government is in a very real sense putting the cart before the horse, because it is not the government that pays for welfare undertakings, but the people themselves. Only for the sake of convenience do we ask the government to redistribute our tax money to us in the form of various benefits. If we grasp this basic fact, I think we will see that before making demands on the government, we must give deep consideration to the question of what benefits are actually needed, while at the same time we must consider how we can improve our conditions through our own efforts.

Who creates our cultural lives?

In our constitution there is only one article referring to the obligation of the people to look to their own well-being; it reads as follows:

> "All people shall have the right to maintain the minimum standards of wholesome and cultured living. In all spheres of life, the State shall use its endeavors for the promotion and extension of social welfare and security, and of public health."

These are excellent provisions, but they are meaningless unless there is a foundation within our society for a healthy cultural life. It seems to me, therefore, that there should be another clause outlining what the people must think and do in order to achieve a higher level of physical and cultural well-being. Whether the authors of the constitution forgot this, or whether they thought it so obvious as not to require mention, they said nothing to the effect that the people are ultimately responsible for their own welfare, as well as their cultural level. Our politicians and our educators remain curiously silent on this point.

Accordingly, few people today consciously realize that if they are to receive welfare benefits or enjoy a higher cultural level, they must work for and pay for this themselves. Moreover, the government and the political parties seem to prefer to ignore this basic truth. Instead, politicians talk constantly about increased social insurance, aid to education, construction of public housing, assistance to small businesses, and the like as though these were favors they were granting to the people out of the goodness of their hearts. It is perhaps only natural, then, that the people have come to expect the government and the politicians automatically to provide them with what they need, or fancy they need, in the way of welfare benefits and cultural improvements. Natural too that the people as a whole tend to relax in the assumption that whether they themselves make an effort or not, somebody will take care of them.

And it works the other way around, too, since the government and the political parties, though presumably aware that they possess no money tree, make promise after promise assuming that the people will supply the taxes necessary to carry out these obligations. In other words, the government and the politicians take it for granted that the people will bail them out in time of need.

What we have then is a whole nation—government, political parties, business enterprises, and the average citizen—relying more or less unconsciously on someone else to do what needs to be done. This is a frightening state of affairs, for when people lose their sense of self-reliance and depend on others, they become weak and helpless. A classic example of the danger entailed is seen in the story of the Battle of Fujikawa, which took place during the twelfth-century wars between the

Minamoto and Taira clans. The Taira had amassed a great army of 100,000 warriors on the banks of the Fujikawa River, but before the battle was joined, the flapping of the wings of waterbirds so frightened the troops that they broke and ran. Think about that for a moment! An army of 100,000 men who, when a few mistook the sound of birds for the coming of the enemy, were completely routed. The trouble was that they were weak in spirit, each of them relying on the strength of others and unable to stand on his own two feet and fight. They were defeated before the battle began.

Dissatisfied youth

Recently, the Office of the Prime Minister conducted a survey among young people in Japan and ten other countries, some of which were advanced industrial nations, and some of which were not. The results showed that dissatisfaction and frustration were more prevalent among youth in Japan than anywhere else. Among the ten countries outside Japan, there were some that almost anybody would consider good places to live, but the majority of them were in many respects not as well-off as Japan. Why is it that the rate of discontent among Japanese young people seems to be higher than among those in these less fortunate countries?

No one, of course, could consider that there is plenty of everything for everybody in Japan today, for the country is still deficient in many respects. On the other hand, a look around the rest of the world is sufficient to show that Japan is relatively affluent. People have an abundance of material possessions; there is more freedom than in many other nations; there are ample opportunities to study; and there are plenty of opportunities for enjoying leisure time. The question of what young people want and like is a serious topic of conversation at many a corporation board meeting. But whether the individual young person will attempt on his own to make up for the things that he feels are missing or ignore all the benefits and complain about the things he does not have depends on whether this individual is self-reliant or fundamentally dependent.

The survey carried out by the Office of the Prime Minister concerned itself with the attitudes of young people, but neither discontent nor dissatisfaction is a monopoly of youth. On the contrary, the young people invariably reflect the adult world, and it is, I think, safe to assume that their discontent is shared by grown people, if not inspired by them. Everywhere in Japan today there is dissatisfaction in the midst of plenty, and this dissatisfaction tends to make people distrustful of anyone they feel to be depriving them of what they want. Distrust creates dissatisfaction, and dissatisfaction breeds distrust—it is a vicious circle. Spiritually, we are probably worse off than we were in the period immediately after the war. In those days we were grateful for anything we received, but now, when we have so much more, we are troubled by not having enough. Furthermore, there is a distinct possibility that our psychological discord could destroy our present affluence, losing for us what we have gained over the years.

We must recover our spirit of independence and self-reliance in the way that our neighor China seems to be trying to do. As the Chinese have no doubt learned, the way of independence is steep and difficult. In the short run, it is easier to rely on others and seek their aid when necessary. There is, however, no assurance that there will in the long run be anybody to rely on. This is the fact that the oil crisis brought home so unmistakably. Ultimately, no path is open to us other than that of self-reliance and independence. Instead of complaining and wallowing in dissatisfaction, let us taste the joy of doing things on our own. Instead of doubting others and criticizing their faults, let us work together as Japanese and as human beings, giving in when necessary to each other, sympathizing with each other, cooperating with each other, and recovering our mutual trust in each other. There is no other way to escape the unrest and uncertainty that beset us today.

Democracy Misunderstood

The sterner aspects of the democratic system

When World War II ended, the people of Japan looked at the world about them and discovered that democracy was the system of government in all of the more advanced countries. In particular, the United States, which was the most prosperous country in the world as well as the nation with which Japan was most closely associated, was of all republics the most democratic, with respect both to government and to ordinary ways of life. It seemed to make sense for Japan also to adopt the democratic system and make it the basis for the reconstruction of our nation. Technically, of course, the democratic system was imposed on Japan by the occupation forces; but its continuance after the occupation testifies to the readiness with which it was accepted. Such opposition as was expressed by certain leaders of the time was largely a matter of details, rather than of broad principles.

We wrote a new constitution in which freedom and

human rights were greatly emphasized, and in general we have abided by that constitution in the ensuing years. This was, I think, a great step forward for Japan. Democratic ideas were by no means completely absent in the prewar years, but they tended to be superficial, and there were many occasions on which civil rights were suppressed or ignored. We are fortunate indeed that we now live and grow in freedom, assured that there are basic rights of which we cannot be deprived.

As I look back over the way in which democracy was introduced and the way in which it has developed, however, I have the feeling that not all of the results have been as favorable as they might have been. This, I think, is because certain features of the democratic system have been misunderstood by most Japanese. Unfortunately, in our original approach to this new system we mistook one aspect for the whole and failed properly to appreciate the remaining aspects. Critics are therefore to some extent right when they say that we imitated the forms without completely grasping the substance. And this failure, I believe, is one of the basic causes of the distrust and frustration that we are experiencing today.

Freedom in society is of the utmost importance. Only when there is freedom can individuals realize their full potentialities, exchange information adequately, and be truly creative. Men cannot live genuinely rewarding lives without freedom, and thus freedom should be maintained as widely as possible. It should go without saying, however, that freedom does not mean the right to do exactly as one pleases, without limits. I have the right of freedom, but so does everyone else, and if I impinge on the freedom of others, then it cannot be said that true freedom exists. As has so often been pointed out, freedom is not the same as license: personal freedom can be recognized only insofar as it does not rob others of freedom, cause damage to them, disturb the life of the community, or stand in the way of the common welfare. True freedom should promote, rather than reduce, harmony in our everyday relations with one another.

Like freedom, human rights are also of the utmost importance. People's rights as individuals and as citizens should be bestowed equally and guarded jealously; but again it is necessary for each person to realize that everyone else has rights too. It is our obligation not only to insist upon our own rights, but to show adequate respect for the rights of others. If we have rights as human beings and rights as citizens, we also have obligations as human beings and obligations as citizens. The two go together, and it is only when this is recognized that true democracy can exist. From both the idealistic and the practical viewpoints, the democratic system has always had a certain element of sternness, as well as an element of permissiveness. For in a democracy, we are all contributing members of a cooperative society; we are the sovereigns who, while maintaining our individual independence, are obliged to look to the maintenance and development of a harmonious communal life.

Some observations on the Japanese constitution

When democracy was instituted in Japan, more attention should have been paid to explaining the duties it entails for the people. Had the obligations of the system been taught by teachers to their students, by leaders to their followers, and by the government to the people, they would certainly be better understood today than they are.

Back in the late 1940's, someone should have declared to the Japanese people, "Democracy is not easy, for in the democratic system we all have obligations to each other. It is on the assumption that these obligations are fulfilled that democracy grants us freedom and civil rights." But in Japan the first part of this somehow got lost, and the people were told, in effect, "Democracy gives us freedom and civil rights, so let's all go out and do exactly what we want to do." Perhaps this is an exaggeration, but it is not far from the truth.

To some extent, the constitution itself is at fault. It contains no less than twenty-seven clauses concerned with rights and privileges, but only three dealing with the obligations of the people. (These three are the obligations to pay taxes, to work, and to educate the young.) Basic human rights are granted, but there is not a word about the duty to respect the basic rights of others. The right to vote is guaranteed, but nothing is said about the duty of the citizen to vote. And, as remarked earlier, the people are assured the right to a minimal standard of health and cultural well-being, but there is no mention of their obligation to cooperate in maintaining this standard.

The constitution, of course, was a product of its time. During the prewar years, so much stress had been laid on the obligations of the people that the authors of the document may well have considered it superfluous to mention them. It must have seemed much more important to specify the basic human rights, which in the past had been ignored or violated.

Once the constitution was in writing, however, it became the foundation for political thought. If our democratic constitution stressed rights and played down obligations, it followed that this was the essence of democracy. Or at least, that is the way most people reasoned, and that is the interpretation of democracy which was taught to the people. Small wonder that today the Japanese people are so greatly concerned with their own rights and so blithely unconcerned with their public obligations. The tendency to do what one pleases, without regard for others, has grown steadily stronger, and the result is that now, whenever people do not get their own way, they consider that they are being deprived of their rights, whether what they want is reasonable from the standpoint of the whole or not.

Social responsibility

In the past few years there has been much talk about the responsibility of business toward the public. In many ways, this is a good thing, because businessmen should at all times be aware of their duties and obligations toward society. They should not be allowed to forget that they have the duty to make and supply the goods the people need, and to do so without violating the people's basic human rights.

At the same time, it should be clearly recognized that business is not the only segment of society that has responsibilities. So do labor unions, schools, religious groups, and political parties, as well as individual politicians, educators, scholars, and religious leaders. Indeed, we all have the responsibility of preserving public morality and of working with each other, as co-sovereigns of the state, to improve our government and our surroundings. To ignore politics is as much a violation of our public responsibility as to litter up the public parks with refuse.

Unfortunately, the tendency is for everyone to worry about everyone else's responsibility and not his own. In my opinion, to question whether or not others are living up to their responsibilities is not in itself bad, for human beings are fallible—prone to ignore their own duties to society unless reminded of them from time to time. It is obvious from the hue and cry one hears today that many people in Japan are vastly concerned over the responsibilities of politicians, businessmen, policemen, schoolteachers, the National Railways, and so on, but it is far from obvious that the average person is concerned over his own responsibilities. Take the case of the schools, for example. Many people pay undercover money to secure places for their children, shrugging their shoulders and saying, "It can't be helped." Don't they realize that in so doing, they themselves are contributing to the inadequacies of the system, rather than working to correct them?

Grass roots

By and large, people grow up to do what they have been taught to do as children. A Japanese child born and brought up in Japan grows up to speak Japanese, just as an English child brought up in England speaks English. On the other hand, a Japanese child brought up where only English is spoken would grow up speaking English, and vice versa.

The main reason why our people have a one-sided view of democracy is that they have never been taught any other view. If in the home, in the school, and in society at large, young people were brought up to believe that while insisting on their rights, they must nevertheless fulfill their obligations in a democratic society, they would learn to do just that, and democracy would truly flourish in our land.

What young people are being taught today, however, is only to insist upon their rights, and as a result they remain largely ignorant of their duties and responsibilities to society. Sooner or later they bump up against somebody whose idea of his rights does not happen to coincide with theirs. Distrust and conflict ensue, and whichever party loses feels mistreated and reacts by hating others, or perhaps by alienating himself from the world.

Adults like myself are quick to deplore this tendency among young people. Still, it would not be fair to castigate the young alone. Educators and political leaders, too, must come in for their share of the blame, and in my opinion it is the lion's share. It is not too late to start teaching the principles of true democracy to the young, but first we must make sure that we understand them ourselves. When we of the adult world have accepted our own responsibilities under the democratic system, and when we have begun to teach genuine democracy to our young, we shall gradually find ourselves surrounded by less discontent and frustration. Education is not accomplished overnight, and it is high time we began again, in the right direction this time.

Whither Japan?

National consciousness

Conflict and warfare continue in the world today. From time to time, international conferences are held to discuss particular problems, but as often as not, they not only fail to arrive at a conclusion or an agreement, but by doing so sow the seeds of still deeper antagonism.

Recently there have been world conferences on the population problem, on natural resources, and on control of the high seas, but none of them has accomplished much, because each nation in attendance was too busy worrying about its own needs to consider those of the other nations. It is not likely that the world will achieve stability or true peace so long as national egos are given full play. Each nation has a right, of course, to see to its own interests, but we have reached a stage where all nations are duty bound to consider the common interests of the world at large.

It seems to me that in comparison with other nations,

Japan today is singularly lacking in national consciousness. By national consciousness, I mean a consciousness of one's country as such and a genuine concern for its well-being—concern such as most people feel for their homes or the communities in which they live. This sentiment, which I consider to be not only legitimate but necessary, is to be distinguished from chauvinism or national selfishness, which can and often does cause conflict and strife, as shown in the world conferences of which I just spoke. We Japanese hardly need be reminded of the potential harm of excessive national self-centeredness, since we are all aware that this was one of the factors that led us into war and defeat. I would be the last to suggest that we need a return to the jingoism of prewar days.

I conceive of national consciousness as consciousness of one's own identity. On a personal level, a man named Yamamoto should understand that he is Yamamoto, and that the blood of his ancestors in the house of Yamamoto runs in his veins. If he does not know whether he is Yamamoto or Tanaka, he can be of very little value to himself or anyone else. In the same way, a Japanese person's sense of his own identity should tell him that he is Japanese and not something else. He should be aware that he was born with a history, a tradition, and certain national traits, and he should try to make the most of them.

On the level of individual human beings, an excessive ego is objectionable; yet there is real need for each person to know exactly who he is and to take care of his interests. Unless one has a sense of one's own identity, one is unable to form true friendships with others or to cooperate with them effectively. It is, ultimately, respect for oneself that enables one to be considerate of others and treat them as they should be treated. A person who holds himself in scorn cannot do this, nor can he command the respect and trust of others.

The same is true of nations. When the people of a nation have a balanced sense of their own importance and are at the same time able to consider the needs of the world as a whole, then they are able to form ties of friendship with other countries and to command the respect of other countries. This is the key to smooth international relations, where nations cooperate with each other for mutual safety and prosperity. The person who has a proper sense of national consciousness naturally expects people in other countries to possess similar feelings. If every nationality were to develop this consciousness and respect the rights of others to have the same, I think we would be much farther along the way to world peace than we are.

If the Japanese people had the proper degree of national consciousness, it would be possible for us to work together to make our country a much more prosperous and livable place than at present. This does not mean that everyone has to have the same opinions, but simply that we should agree on the need to work together for the common good. We would then have a sense of unity that would restore mutual confidence and put an end to fruitless recriminations and internal strife.

Foreign observers seem to feel that Japanese already have a strong sense of nationality, and in one sense I suppose they are correct. Japan is, after all, a country with a two-thousand-year history, and there are very few other countries in which a single people has lived and thrived for so long. Many Japanese who pride themselves on their internationalism nonetheless possess a sense of nationality which, in times of stress, they are apt to fall back on. This, however, is entirely different from the sense of basic unity with the remainder of the Japanese people, the willingness to work together, with which I am concerned.

At present, the Japanese public is seriously, even dangerously, fragmented. Every individual and every group appears to be out solely for his or its own ends, like the nations at the international conferences. There is a saying to the effect that "brothers may fight, but when reviled by strangers, they stick together." However, this is no longer true in Japan. On the contrary, Japanese today constantly use criticisms from abroad as weapons against their domestic adversaries. Indeed, many of them deliberately carry their internal quarrels abroad to seek aid and abetment from foreign nations. Fighting together uncompromisingly as we do, we could easily all go down together in the face of some threat from without. The only cure for this situation is to regain a proper concern for the good of the nation as a whole.

I do not mean by this that the individual Japanese should invariably put the nation's interests ahead of his own. On the contrary, this would invite the same sort of ultranationalism that we had before. And yet, with a proper sense of national consciousness, a person can see that in a broad way the nation's interest and his own are bound to coincide, for unless the individual people of the country enjoy increasing benefits and happiness, the country itself cannot be said to prosper or develop, and when the country is in a state of confusion and instability, it is difficult for individuals to find either material benefit or spiritual peace of mind. In this respect, there arise occasions when the individual must subject his own interests to those of the country as a whole. But there are also instances in which the individual must insist upon greater respect for his own needs. Ideally, there should be harmony rather than domination between the interests of the nation and those of the individual.

Today it seems to me that the Japanese sense of national consciousness is growing weaker. One can see this, for instance, in the attitude of a good part of the people toward the national flag and the national anthem. Nowadays, Japanese schools only rarely raise the national flag, and when they do, there is invariably opposition from a number of teachers and parents. The students thus learn that there is something faintly wicked about raising the national flag or singing the national anthem.

I was impressed some time ago, as I watched a political demonstration in America on television, to see that the American flag was carried in the vanguard of the procession. This, I think, is right and as it should be. Nothing could be more natural to a people with a sense of national consciousness. In the newly independent countries, either leftist or rightist, the people are quick to adopt national flags and anthems, and their leaders try very hard to create a sense of national unity. That after two thousand years of history it is impossible in Japan today to fly the flag or sing the national anthem without being criticized is evidence that something is wrong with our sense of ourselves as a nation.

The present situation is due to some extent to the influence of the occupation forces. Broadly speaking, the occupation personnel as a whole considered the prewar nationalism of Japan to have been the cause of the war in the Pacific. As I have indicated above, there was indeed an element of fanaticism in the prewar concept of the nation, and the country was in those times prone to regard only its own interests. At the same time, it seems to me that in that era the same tendency existed in most of the other countries of the world, and that Japan was by no means alone in having an exaggerated pride. This was eliminated after the war, as it should have been. But in the process of eliminating it, we sometimes went too far in the opposite direction. At one stage, for example, the teaching of Japanese history was actually dropped from the public school curriculum.

The occupation forces were right in trying to eradicate fanatic nationalism, but insofar as they attempted to eliminate national consciousness altogether, they were mistaken. This was simply throwing out the baby with the bath water. It remains for us now to rekindle a proper sense of national consciousness and by doing so to promote peace and friendship, not only within Japan, but throughout the world as a whole.

Political mollycoddling

It seems to me that if we are to acquire a proper sense of national consciousness, the government must accept a leading role in creating it. We need more leaders who actually lead, and who are able to inspire in the people a sense of national pride—not a vague mystique of the sort prevalent before the war, but honest pride in real accomplishments. The reason why we have no such leadership at present is that our politicians lack a philosophy. Our political leaders as a whole, both liberals and conservatives, have no clear concept of what our country should be like twenty-five or a hundred years hence.

In the thirty years since the war, we have lacked the sort of political leadership that would be capable of issuing the call for nationwide reassessment now necessary. Instead, our politicians have busied themselves coddling the people along, telling them what they would like to hear. They understand that they must attract votes to be elected, and all of them, government party and opposition alike, seem to have concluded that it is easier to attract votes by sweet-talking the people than by providing genuine leadership. They promise the people this, then they promise the people that, and by and by the people are led to believe that social insurance, educational benefits, housing, aid to small business, and so on will be dispensed to them like candy from a paper sack.

President Kennedy's outlook

I am reminded, in this connection, of the injunction President John Kennedy issued to the American people in his Inaugural Address. He said, "Ask not what your country can do for you. Ask what you can do for your country!" It seems to me that his words show a perfect grasp of the proper relationship between the government and the people in a democratic nation. It is, I think, the essence of democracy for people to ask themselves what they can do for themselves before they make demands upon the government. It is this sort of initiative that creates a solid foundation for the nation and makes possible a high level of development. President Kennedy showed true greatness in making this appeal to the people at the very beginning of his administration.

What we need from the Japanese government now is the same sort of frankness that President Kennedy displayed. The people are not stupid: from time to time they can be lulled into complacency with promises and mollycoddling, but most of them would respond favorably to a true and just appeal. These are not ordinary times. The country is on the road to collapse, and I suspect that the people as a whole would be grateful to hear an appeal that had the ring of truth about it. I think they would like to hear the facts, even if this entailed a scolding or discomfort. Our government and political parties owe us a strictly realistic statement as to where we stand.

No philosophical bearings

As to why no plea like President Kennedy's has been issued to the Japanese people, I can only conclude that it is because of the lack among our politicians of a long-term concept of the direction in which Japan should move. There exists no fixed criterion for deciding what should be done in any given situation. Instead, there is a strong tendency toward deciding everything that comes up on a case-by-case basis. For lack of a fundamental guideline, the politicians are unable to stand up before the people and tell them where the people have failed to toe the line. It is so much easier to attract votes by flattering and indulging the electors' whims.

A country lacking a basic philosophy is like an individual with no sure outlook on life, like a corporation or a shop with no concept of managerial policy. An individual without a basic philosophy of life is unable to judge the good or bad points of the people with whom he comes in contact, and is consequently unable to associate with them on equal terms. He grovels before those who are strong and lords it over those who are weak. A corporation without basic principles is incapable of strong management. It stumbles from one phase of the economic cycle to the next, never able to advance very far without soon retreating. Typically, a company of this sort is unable to train new people and thereby ensure its own future development.

A country without a basic philosophy is like such a company multiplied many times over. Its policies lack consistency, and the activities of its people seem to go in all directions at once. There is always a certain feeling of weakness and uncertainty. If I may be allowed the analogy, the people now aboard the *S. S. Japan* are wondering which way their ship is headed. It lurches to the east, then it swings to the west, and all the passengers can do is hang on for dear life. Everyone is out for himself, and what one person does is almost immediately undone by somebody else. No one's effort has the effect it was expected to have, and the net result is waste and inefficiency.

In the long run, all of the difficulties confronting us now derive from the lack of any philosophy as to how the country should be run. If, for example, we had a definite set of principles, it would be relatively simple to decide how to manage our schools and educate our young people. As it is, however, that most vital of our activities, the training of our youth, is being conducted in a haphazard fashion. Moreover, much of the discontent and dissatisfaction expressed by the young results from the absence of a clear-cut national philosophy; for the point that troubles these young people is that they cannot find for themselves a definite goal, either for studying, or for working, or for just living.

This is not true to the same extent in other countries, regardless of their system of government. One may or may not approve of the governmental philosophy of China, or the Soviet Union, or many of the developing nations, but at least those countries have philosophies, and they are managing their affairs in accordance with them.

The *S. S. Japan*, with 110,000,000 aboard, has encountered a typhoon and is on the verge of sinking. Some of the people are running back and forth on deck in great confusion; others are brawling with each other over who is responsible for the storm; still others, below deck and unaware of the danger, are lost in dreams of clear skies and fair weather. What all the passengers have in common is that not one of them knows which way the *S. S. Japan* is sailing. Unless something is done, the ship will drift off into oblivion and capsize. When that happens, everyone will go down with it.

This is no time to be dreaming of clear skies or squabbling amongst ourselves. It is a time to join hands and try to save the ship, and the first step we must take is to decide upon a national philosophy that will determine which way the *S. S. Japan* will steer.

Part II: Meeting the Challenge

Thoughts on Education

Are we prepared?

I believe that there is a way out of our political muddle and spiritual impasse—a way that would not only enable us to avoid calamity, but simultaneously make it possible for us to create a nation so well run that it would serve as a model to the rest of the world.

To do this, as I have stated, we must undergo major surgery to remove our country's ailments by the roots. And it is to the roots that we must go, or else we run the risk of losing an arm or a leg to no avail. Nor will the operation be painless, for despite the anesthetics that modern medicine has developed, it is still impossible for a human being to undergo major surgery without a certain amount of pain, and the same will be true to an even greater extent in the case of surgery on the body of a whole nation. Indeed, the pain will be felt, in one way or another, by our entire populace. The question is whether we are prepared to face it or not.

If the people shrink from pain, if they try to flee from

the inevitable, then there is nothing left for us but to sink together. If, on the other hand, everyone is prepared to bear his share of the pain, to grit his teeth and endure for a few years, the country can be saved. We must have determination in order to survive. And if we do, I believe the operation will be successful.

Too much of a good thing

We must first insert the scalpel into education, I think, for the problems in our education system have ramifications extending into nearly every phase of our social and economic life. In my opinion, it would not be unjust to say that Japan today is following an educational policy that will lead straight to ruin. No doubt the country's educators will resent me for saying this, and their indignation would be understandable, for it has been through their efforts over the years that education has become probably more widespread in Japan than in any other country while at the same time reaching a very high level of quality.

I would be the first to agree that by most existing standards Japanese education today is very thorough. What concerns me, however, is not a deficiency in our educational system, but rather the possibility that we have carried a good thing too far. Specifically, because of overemphasis on the importance of diplomas and degrees, we are attempting, at great expense to the public, to administer higher education where it is neither needed nor desired.

There is an old saying to the effect that "to do too much is not to do enough." If a person suffers from malnutrition, it is necessary to feed him well, but if he is already well nourished, it is not good to continue stuffing him with food. I believe that education in Japan today is being overnourished, and it seems to me that we must institute basic reforms to create a system of education that is better suited to the actual living standards of our people and to our country's real capacities, as opposed to its ideas or pretensions.

Part of our difficulty arises from mistakes that were made during the early postwar period, when a tendency was born to disregard the question of whether an expansive education program could be carried out within our means. Before the war, Japan had what is sometimes described as a six-five-six school system. The first six years consisted of primary schooling, which was obligatory. This was followed by five years of middle school for some children, then six years of college. In addition, there were two- and three-year programs of advanced primary schooling for children who wanted a little more education without setting out on the road to college or the professions, as well as professional schools of three years or more for graduates of middle school.

In 1947, at the instigation of the occupation forces, an education reform was carried out, and the prewar system was replaced by the six-three-three-four system, which is still in effect today. With this arrangement, there are six years of primary school, three years of junior high school, three years of high school, and four years of college. The first nine years, which involve primary school and junior high school, are compulsory.

The prewar Japanese school system was set up in the Meiji era (1868–1912). In that age, the leaders of Japan were eager to modernize the nation, and they regarded the education of the people as a necessary step toward this goal. They studied the school systems employed in the various countries of Europe and adopted such features from them as they deemed applicable to Japan. As in other fields of culture, a school system based on what was considered to be the most advanced in foreign countries was adopted and then Japanized. Over the years the system was further modified now and then to accord with changing conditions, and there arose, I believe, a school structure that fitted the needs of Japan at the time.

The Meiji-era school system was designed to train all the various kinds of individuals needed in a modern industrial society. It is true that the number of positions at the top of the educational ladder were limited and tended to be monopolized by the sons of the elite who could afford not to put children to work for the length of time required for the university. Still, the system was based upon the idea of supplying as much education as possible within society's means; and it was worked out pragmatically. Hence, when it became clear that society could afford to extend compulsory education from the original four years to six, this was done.

I am not at all certain that there was any need to subject the prewar system to wholesale revision after the war. It would have been better, I think, to adopt a gradual approach, revising the system a little at a time as needed. No doubt the switch to a democratic form of government made it necessary to eliminate the element of elitism that existed in the prewar schools. Nevertheless, if it had been decided after due deliberation that a sweeping revision was necessary, it ought to have been undertaken in a more cautious fashion, with more time allowed for adequate preparation and groundwork.

The procedure whereby the new system was actually instituted can hardly be described as anything but precipitous. In March, 1946, less than a year after the war ended, the first Mission on Education came from the United States to visit Japan. A Japanese committee, previously set up on orders from the Supreme Commander, cooperated with the American group in carrying out a one-month survey of Japanese eduation. On the basis of this quick study, a report was drawn up on educational policy, and this became the basis for the new school system, which was inaugurated in April of the following year. The new school structure had much to recommend it, and it has worked admirably in some respects. But the manner in which it came into being was questionable, to say the least.

In the first place, it was a mistake, I think, to start from the assumption that the prewar Japanese educational system was in itself bad. The Allied occupation forces, and particularly the Americans, seemed to think at the time that prewar education was one of the chief reasons for Japan's having gone to battle, and that therefore education should be radically changed. It was true, no doubt, that the content of prewar education was in some ways excessively nationalistic, and perhaps it was only natural that foreign observers would consider the fault to lie in the system itself. It is also true, I think, that the American educators who advocated the new system did so for the purpose of making Japan a better nation and of contributing to the cause of peace. Still, I think it undeniable that the reformers overlooked the better features of the prewar system, in particular its pragmatic nature. I have been told, too, that the Mission on Education was composed to a large degree of progressives who favored reforms that had not even been tried in the United States, and that as a result of their efforts, the new Japanese system had an unduly idealistic aspect.

Education, of course, must be carried out with ideals in mind, so that idealism in this respect is not of itself to be condemned. And yet, when idealism outstrips reality, problems are bound to arise. In this instance, the danger was multiplied by the speed with which the Japanese authorities accepted the recommendations. With only a year of preparation for the adoption of a completely new system, which involved nearly doubling existing educational facilities and personnel, it would have been miraculous if everything had subsequently gone smoothly. Indeed, thirty years later, it seems in many ways remarkable that the new system yielded no more confusion than it did.

When the new school program was adopted, there were educators, even in America, who questioned Japan's ability to carry out the transformation called for, particularly with the Japanese economy in a state of depletion. It may be considered that Japan's ability to make the new system work, somehow, was a result of Japanese tradition; after all, the nation had for centuries been adopting cultural elements from other countries and managing in one way or another to digest them.

In postwar West Germany, the situation was different, for even though the nation was under occupation its leaders absolutely rejected a sweeping educational reform. As a result of their stubbornness and their subsequent efforts gradually to remold existing conditions, the present system is well suited to Germany's needs and social conditions, and it is operating very smoothly. It is Japan's misfortune, I think, that its leaders were unable after the war to muster the prudence demonstrated by their German counterparts, for the drastic nature of the postwar educational reform created imbalances that have tended to grow worse rather than to resolve themselves—especially with respect to higher education, as I will elaborate below.

With regard to the extension of compulsory education from six years to nine, I have no great quarrel. This was at the time a very expensive undertaking for a defeated country, but in this instance social and economic conditions adjusted themselves to the ideal in a relatively short time. Indeed, at present I think it might be feasible to reduce the age for school entrance by one year and offer ten, rather than nine, years of compulsory schooling. This is not to say, however, that I agree with the substance of compulsory education as it has developed since the educational reform.

There are many theories as to what should be taught in a program of compulsory education, but I believe that the basic aim should be to teach children how to be people, or in other words to give them the basic knowledge and sense of values needed to survive and be useful in life. They must, of course, be given physical training and be taught to read and calculate as well, for these things are fundamental. But in a broader sense, the education program should aim at teaching them the ways of acting, the ways of thinking, and the ways of making judgments that they need in order to become well-rounded human beings functioning in a communal society. In the very early stages of their education, when they are still quite young and impressionable, they should be given the moral training needed for ordinary human life. Nor should this training be merely a rote-like process in which they learn in the abstract about the rules of good manners or the need for mutual love among men. The emphasis must be on the actual practice of moral principles. When such a foundation has been laid, it can serve as a basis for future intellectual development.

In order to bring such results about, I would suggest certain operational changes in our primary school education. In the first place, I think that the present primary and junior high schools should be combined, and, as suggested earlier, that the length of compulsory education should be increased from nine to ten years. If this were done, I think there should be a fairly clear division made between the first five years and the second; the first five years should be devoted more thoroughly to the type of human training I have been discussing, while the second five years could then be spent in implementing this training and in imparting a higher degree of intellectual knowledge. In my opinion, this type of division suits the training to the age level of the children.

Under the present system, the functions of primary and junior high schools are defined and divided, but there is a vagueness about the purpose of each. In particular, in many respects junior high school has come to be no more than a place where children learn to pass examinations for high school. This, of course, is not merely a fault of the system, and it will not be eliminated unless we have a basic revolution in our attitudes toward education as a whole. I do not believe that a mere revision of the school structure without a change in values would solve all our problems, but the change I have suggested might be a viable way of bringing our program of compulsory education into better line with social realities.

My reason for stressing the defects of our compulsory school programs is that they arise in large measure from our excesses at the higher educational levels. Our current urge to send more and more people to high schools and colleges has led inevitably to a situation in which compulsory schooling has come to be considered not as a preparation for living, but as a preparation for higher schooling. The consequences to the nation are perilous, because we have many, many young people who emerge from the compulsory program not knowing what they ought to know, knowing a good deal they will never need, and, in all too many instances, feeling deprived or in some way inferior because they cannot for one reason or another go on to the higher schools they wish to attend.

Too many universities

The postwar educational reform, which was aimed in part at reducing the relative importance of traditional universities operated by the national government, led to a proliferation of prefectural and private universities. If we except the professional high schools and junior colleges, in 1935 there were forty-five colleges and universities throughout the country, having a total enrollment of 69,000 students. Today there are no fewer than four hundred colleges with 1,600,000 students—in other words, nine times as many colleges and twenty times as many students as forty years ago. Furthermore, the number of high school graduates who enter college is no less than thirty percent of the total.

I submit that this is too many colleges and too many college students for Japan in its present state of socio-economic development. Fundamentally, we are spending more than we can afford to produce college graduates whom our society cannot adequately absorb. What is the sense in having graduates of college who drive taxis for a living, as some indeed do today? Far from needing a college education to drive a taxi, a person would be better off to quit school after junior high or high school and take up driving. That way, he would learn to drive at an earlier age, do his work better, and contribute in his own way to the public welfare. Moreover, if he happened to be one of the many young men who were pushed through college by their families against their own inclination, he would probably be happier.

The case of the college-educated taxi driver is perhaps extreme, but there are hosts of other college graduates employed in work that neither requires a college education nor can provide a sense of usefulness for young men and women who have one. Companies hire them because they are readily available, because they are presumably of superior intelligence, because they normally have a certain veneer that high school graduates lack, because their college connections may come in handy in the future, and because other companies hire them. Unless they are technicians, they normally spend their first few years doing work that could easily be done by a high school graduate, though for higher salaries than high school graduates command. All this is extremely uneconomical, of course; but the added cost is normally invisible to begin with, and it is not high enough in any case to move many companies to buck the system. Still, this is one of those wasteful, inefficient practices that contribute to inflation.

There are today about a hundred and fifty countries in the world, and conditions, as well as standards of living, vary from each to the next. It is possible, for example, that one particular country is strong enough economically and sufficiently developed culturally to sustain a level of thirty percent in the rate of advancement of high school graduates to college. At the same time, this level might well be too high for another country, in which case an attempt to maintain such a level might well cause serious damage to the economy and the social fabric. The latter country might find upon reflection that the level suited to its capabilities is twenty percent, or ten, or even five. It is important, I think, to aim just a little high: if a level of ten percent is considered appropriate, a country should aim at eleven percent. But it should not try in one swoop to jump to the highest level prevailing in other countries, or else it will soon find itself spending too much on education and thereby creating internal rifts.

The figures are not fixed, of course. As countries develop, conditions naturally change, and it may well happen that a country currently able to sustain a level of only five percent will be able in fifty years to support a level of thirty percent. The important point is to suit the level, as well as the rate of progress, to conditions actually existing in the country in question. It would appear that this is what is actually being done in such countries as the United States, the Soviet Union, and West Germany. In Japan, however, considerations of this sort were thrown to the four winds when the postwar educational reform was carried out. For at that time we adopted essentially the same system that was employed in the United States, a country with vastly greater economic means. At the lower levels, we have somehow adjusted, but at the higher levels we are still saddled with a much larger apparatus than we require.

It is said that the level of education in Japan today is second only to that of the United States. And yet it is symptomatic of the laxness and wastefulness of the Japanese system that nearly every student who enters college graduates, whereas in America, I am told, the study requirements in the colleges are such that only about half of the entrants manage to graduate.

Moreover, the brute fact is that an appallingly large proportion of our college graduates acquire all or nearly all of the academic knowledge they possess prior to their entrance into college. One could argue that in Japan we are merely creating places where it is possible to become educated while paying too little attention to the actual substance of education. In this respect, our system is extraordinarily luxurious and wasteful.

It behooves us, I think, to follow the lead of America, the Soviet Union, and West Germany and to reform our education system in such a way as to render it suitable to conditions that actually obtain in our country. Personally, I think Japan could and should reduce the number of colleges and high schools by approximately half. This reduction need not necessarily be permanent, for it may be that in ten or twenty years, we will have overcome the problems that now exist and grown in cultural and spiritual abundance to the extent that we need a larger system. That would be excellent. Still, at the present time, when attending college seems to increase rather than to alleviate the students' sense of injustice and frustration, thus adding to our social difficulties, I think we should have fewer colleges.

Actually, by "half" I mean "an appropriate figure," for a thorough study might indicate that the needed reduction is less or more. My experience leads me to believe that half would be about right, and I use that proportion for purposes of argument; but I am primarily concerned with putting across the idea that we need a substantial reduction, as opposed to a continued cancerous growth.

Abolish the University of Tokyo?

Some of my readers will, I suspect, say that I am behind the times when I advocate a reduction in educational facilities, but I ask these dissenters to think my proposals over calmly and objectively, even if they go against the grain. I have thought about the matter a good deal myself, and I make these suggestions because I think they would make life happier and more fruitful for the young people themselves. Let us never forget that it is these youngsters who must find real meaning in life in order to accept the responsibilities of a future age.

What I am saying, quite simply, is that the number of high school students entering college should be reduced from thirty percent to about fifteen, thus making it possible to reduce the number of state and private colleges by half. In the process, we would limit college attendance to those who are truly qualified and truly desirous of learning. One result would certainly be that the value of a college education would be increased, and another no doubt would be that teachers would be better qualified than they are at present.

A third result would be a great financial saving to the country. I do not by any means wish to suggest that educational reforms should be undertaken for the sole purpose of saving money. And yet it is important to take into account that great savings would result. As to the amounts involved, let us consider, for example, what would happen if the University of Tokyo were closed down.

Now, the University of Tokyo is one of the world's great institutions of learning, and even if half of the universities in the country were abolished, it would no doubt be preserved. Still, it is interesting to consider the hypothetical economic effect of shutting it down, for it costs the Japanese government on the order of fifty billion yen ($170,000,000) a year to operate. To eliminate this expenditure would be no small saving in itself, but we must also take into consideration that the University of Tokyo has land, facilities, and other properties that by a conservative estimate must be worth something like one trillion yen ($3,300,000,000). If these possessions were sold off to the public at the price named, and the interest on the proceeds calculated at ten percent per year, the resulting income or savings to the government per annum would be one hundred billion yen ($330,000,000). Adding to this the previous fifty billion yen in operating costs, we find that closing the University of Tokyo would save the Japanese government about one hundred and fifty billion yen ($500,000,000) each year.

If this sum were used to make possible an income tax reduction for low-income families, it should be possible to exempt six or seven million people from taxes altogether. And if abolishing the University of Tokyo would make it possible for six or seven million people to be relieved of taxes, it follows that at present six or seven million people are being taxed solely for the purpose of running the University of Tokyo.

The University of Tokyo is only one of about a hundred national universities, colleges, and junior colleges, which together require an annual expenditure of around five hundred billion yen ($1,700,000,000). In addition, the government dispenses a total of approximately seventy billion yen ($225,000,000) in aid and subsidies to two or three hundred private universities. If the number of colleges and universities were halved, then, the direct annual saving to the government would be on the order of three hundred billion yen ($1,000,000,000). In addition, if the properties of the government institutions were disposed of and the interest on the proceeds figured at ten percent, as above, the total annual saving to the government would amount to some two trillion yen ($6,700,000,000) per year, which would make it possible to eliminate income taxes for about 24,000,000 people or, in lieu of that, to provide a much improved program of public welfare.

Cutting the number of high schools

As I stated above, I also advocate cutting the number of

high schools in half. For this, I am sure I will be criticized even more harshly than in the case of the universities, especially since there are already many people in favor of making high school compulsory. As an ideal for the future, I too would be in favor of compulsory high school education, though not in the form in which it is now offered, and certainly not now, when we are in the worst national crisis we have ever faced. Our problem at this time is not under-education, but over-education or inefficient education, and I believe that halving the number of high schools would be an important step toward making Japan a better and wiser country, rather than the opposite. Actually, since high schools today are in many ways no more than preparatory schools for students aiming at college, a reduction in their number is no more than a logical consequence of reducing the number of colleges.

I believe that we might do well to give further thought to the five-year period between the time when a young person completes his compulsory education and the time when he is recognized as an adult. At present, when a person reaches the age of twenty, he suddenly acquires the rights, privileges, and obligations of an adult. Overnight, certain things that were forbidden become permissible, and vice versa. This sink- -or-swim approach is one way of handling the transition, but might it not be better to have a period of preparation for the shock of becoming adult?

In the Japan of the past, when a boy reached the age of about thirteen or fourteen, he was considered to have come of age and a celebration was held to commemorate this event. Thereafter, the boy was treated as an adult, and in the premodern period, he was expected to become a soldier in times of war. The situation is very different today, but I suspect we should still recognize that at the age of about fifteen young people begin to become adults. We might, I think, consider the age between fifteen and twenty as a transitional stage in which young people are "apprentice adults." During this interval, they might receive to some extent the protection normally provided for children, but at the same time be given certain responsibilities and privileges of adulthood. They would learn gradually to think of themselves as adults, and we would be entitled to expect them to act more like adults.

During the first two or three years of this transitional stage, we might consider a type of compulsory education different in nature from that given to children and far less oriented to the needs of those planning to enter college. This education would be the responsibility of the nation, and once it was completed, the individual young person would have the freedom to continue or not continue his formal schooling. Before adopting such a system, of course, we would need a period of, say, ten years of preparation, during which teachers could be trained to implement the program. For the moment, I think, the more urgent need is to trim down our highly inflated high school system.

Most of our present high schools are public, which means that they are run at the expense of local governments. The amount spent by the local governments on high school education each year is nearly one trillion yen ($3,300,000,000). By halving the number of high schools, then, the local governments would save something on the order of five hundred billion yen ($1,670,000,000) annually, which would make it possible for these governments, which are currently operating at a deficit, to provide needed welfare benefits and public improvements that cannot now be financed.

Again, the principal aim in reducing the number of schools would not be to save money, but to insure that the right people go to high school. At present, more than ninety percent of our young people attend high school, and I feel certain that, as in the case of the colleges, at least a third of them go to school only because it is considered the thing to do. It is very clear from everything one sees, hears, or reads that in present-day Japan neither parents nor children are stopping to consider whether attending high school is really the best thing for an individual child's future. Education is simply treated as a sacred cow.

Taken all in all, I think it would be better for our children and for society as a whole if, when a child finished compulsory junior high school, he were given a chance to decide for himself which path he wants to follow. He should not be pressured to opt for high school, and he should certainly not be made to feel that unless he goes, he is in some way inferior to others.

Today, one result of the high rate of high school attendance is that we have a shortage of young people trained in various manual skills and in the crafts. It is very difficult, for example, to find a young person who is skilled as a plasterer, or a carpenter, or a mechanic, or a practitioner of one of the traditional handicrafts. The reason is that the best time to learn such skills is when the person is fourteen or fifteen, and today just about all young people of that age are in school. This shortage of skilled young men is particularly serious, because it is one of the most important direct causes of high prices.

We need more nurses

At present, for example, it is said that the sewage system in Tokyo is approximately one hundred years behind that of Paris. To bring it up to date would require the expenditure of several trillions of yen, but as of now the work could not be undertaken even if the funds and supplies were available, for there is no one to do the work. And because there is no one to do the work, the price of all the machinery and materials required will doubtless be higher when the work is eventually done than it is now. This is the sort of phenomenon I had in mind when I said we were following an educational policy that leads straight to national ruination. I do not think the phrase is an overstatement.

For lack of young men, construction companies, especially in the countryside, must rely on middle-aged women who are no longer tied to the home; this is both a dangerous and an inefficient practice in an accident-prone industry. Work of the sort involved in civil engineering should obviously be done by strong, healthy young men to begin with, but the strong, healthy young men are all away in college. Quite a few of them, no doubt, are studying hard to become useful and productive members of society, but there are many others who spend their time playing mah-jongg or smashing up things with their wooden staffs and steel bars. Why, I ask, should prices not go up?

The shortage of young labor extends throughout the country and its effects are varied. In many small businesses, for instance, owners or managers are forced to do work that ought to be done by young boys or girls, because the young boys and girls are simply unavailable. A delivery boy of seventeen or eighteen can make deliveries better and faster than a shopowner of forty or fifty, and when the shopowner, for the lack of a boy, must deliver his own goods, there is a corresponding loss of efficiency. The loss is all the greater because the shopowner is not free to do his own work. In this way, productivity is being reduced in many shops and companies, and the result is higher costs in both manufacture and sales. Increased expenses arise in every phase of a company's work, and it is inevitable that prices must go up. The lack of young people to do work that can and ought to be done by young people is one of the more important causes of inflation today.*

From this viewpoint, it would be a good idea, I think, after the number of colleges and high schools is reduced to half, to replace some of them with professional and trade schools, such as, for example, nursing schools. The reason why I chose this example is that in many hospitals today beds and whole wards are going unused for lack of nurses. Government regulations require that a certain number of nurses must be on duty for a given number of beds, and there simply are not enough nurses to go around. This is a great burden on many hospitals, not to speak of their patients or would-be patients. As it stands now, in order to become a registered nurse, the candidate must attend a nursing school for three years after finishing high school. A number of doctors have assured me, however, that it would be better to send the students to nursing school immediately after junior high school. They say the students learn faster that way, and of course with the added three years of actual experience, they become expert nurses more quickly. If the law were rewritten so that

*By the spring of 1975, unemployment in Japan was distinctly on the rise, but this has not altered the basic situation described here, for the bulk of the unemployed are older workers.

young people out of junior high school could go directly to nursing school, we would have more nurses, fewer vacant hospital beds, and perhaps fewer sick people. This is only one example, but similar considerations apply to professional schools in many other fields.

Actually, with respect to vocational training to replace the present high schools, rather than have the government become involved in some large expansion program, I think it would be far better to explore the possibilities of private efforts in this field. One alternative would be the age-old method of letting young people go out into society to find older people to train them. A second would be for business to provide educational facilities, in which case the curriculum need not necessarily be limited to what is generally thought of as occupational training.

When I was a child, most doctors had assistants who did a good deal of medical work. These were, as a rule, people who wanted to become doctors, but who did not have the funds to attend medical college. They hired themselves out as live-in assistants and studied medicine while aiding their employers on actual medical cases. Eventually many of them passed the national examination for medical practitioners and became doctors on their own. In the past, many excellent doctors learned their profession in this fashion, without going through a formal course of training in a medical school.

Today, medicine is far more advanced than it was in those days, and it would be difficult to employ exactly the same system. But the general idea could be applied to a greater extent than it is now, not only in the field of medicine, but in many other professions. If it were applied, school training could be held to the necessary minimum, and professional standards could be upheld by a system of qualifying examinations. This would, in my opinion, cost less money and be more effective than the method now in use.

We in Japan should not forget, I think, that in the Meiji era, training methods of this sort actually succeeded in converting Japan from an underdeveloped nation into a modern one. Today, when people everywhere have come to accept the notion that education is the government's responsibility, it would be healthy, I believe, for us to reconsider the accomplishments of an earlier age in which people were less dependent upon the state.

Business should also take a more active role in education. By this I do not mean merely on-the-job training in the normal sense, but rather a broader type of schooling which companies would provide for their employees or apprentice-employees. In my opinion, the establishment of schools by business concerns should be encouraged, and steps should be taken to provide students who have completed such schooling with appropriate qualifications and credentials.

Before the war, we had within my company a school called the Employee Training Institute. Here, graduates of primary schools were given a three-year course in which they covered the commercial and industrial courses provided by the old middle schools while at the same time working at their jobs. Suitable training of a liberal arts nature was also included, with the aim of producing graduates who were skilled not only in their jobs, but in the science of living. The school had to be closed during the war, but it is gratifying today to see that many of its graduates are now outstanding executives in our company.

After the war, we attempted something similar in the form of the Matsushita Electric Institute of Engineering, in which graduates of the new junior high schools were qualified for enrollment. Because of changed social conditions, however, this school was not a success. Specifically, the number of junior high school graduates who went on to high school increased at such a rapid rate that our school became superfluous, particularly since it was not allowed to give its graduates diplomas. I am sure that the school offered fully as good academic and practical training as the ordinary high school, but it did not qualify as one. With more and more junior high graduates going to high school, applications fell off, and today the institute's facilities are used not for their original purpose but for the reeducation of older employees.

In the prewar days there were many young men and women who, though possessing the necessary intelligence and ability, were unable to go beyond primary school. For that reason, not only my company but also many others maintained educational facilities of their own, and there were many applicants for the training programs offered. The company schools were a boon not only to those who attended them, but to the companies that ran them and to society as a whole.

Today, however, just about everybody can go to high school, and young people are no longer interested in company educational programs that do not lead to a diploma. This, I think, is unfortunate for the young people, for business, and for the nation. The situation could be altered very simply by allowing company schools to qualify as high schools and to give high school diplomas. Companies operating such schools should, for their part, agree not to retain all the graduates, but to release half of them for employment elsewhere.

If this were done, it would be possible for many young people to receive diplomas while at the same time acquiring the knowledge and skill needed for a profession. This combination would, I think, be attractive to a large number of young people. It would also provide business with a source of well-trained people, and I believe that businesses in general would be happy to release graduates above a certain level as a contribution to society. Such a plan, without costing the government one yen, would implement our education facilities, provide satisfaction for many young people, and also raise the general level of occupational training.

At present, there are about two million young people

in colleges of one sort or another and four million in high school. The measure I am proposing would, therefore, convert about three million youths from pure consumers into producers, and this in itself would certainly make for the stabilization of prices. Furthermore, if the young people were allowed to do what they are most fit to do, whether it be work or study, there would be much less frustration and dissatisfaction among them, for the psychological strain that burdens so many of them would be reduced. Over and above this, the vast amount of money saved by the national and local governments could be used to stabilize prices, implement public facilities, and provide greater welfare benefits for the people.

It should not be overlooked that closing half of the colleges and high schools would make available a large amount of land and many physical facilities. Land now owned by private schools that would be closed might be bought up by the government and, together with the land from the public schools, be converted into parks or other installations needed by the people as a whole. This would help provide more playgrounds for our children and make possible any number of recreational facilities that cannot now be built for want of space.

Teachers' salaries

Reducing the number of schools by half would, as we

have seen, enable us to kill three or four birds with one stone; but in enumerating all the good features, we should not neglect certain difficulties that would doubtless arise. It is certain, for example, that if half the young people found themselves unable to attend high school or college, many of them would be unhappy, and some would feel deprived of their right to gain academic qualifications. Such people deserve our ample consideration, not only morally, but from the practical viewpoint. It seems to me that for the benefit of these young people, the government could arrange to hold three or four times each year national examinations through which it would be possible to receive a high school diploma, a college degree, or even a doctorate without having received the customary formal education.

Since most Japanese businesses either have shifted or are shifting to a five-day week, workers now have a good deal of spare time in which to study or make use of the many existing facilities for self-education. Objectively speaking, there is ample opportunity for young people to study if they are so inclined, and many of them would doubtless find that they could acquire a high school diploma in five or six years while working, and then perhaps go on to a college degree. I think, too, that quite a few superior students might well be able to earn a high school diploma and a college degree in less than the seven years now required. I do not, of course, offer this as the absolute ideal, for the ideal would be to build a Japan in which everyone who wants to and has the requisite ability could go to high school and college or beyond, without restriction of number. The more urgent problem at the moment, however, is to save our country from collapse, and until we have done so, the suggestion I have made would, I think, serve as a plan for the transition.

The people who would be hardest hit by the closure of half the schools would be the teachers, of whom there are currently nearly 380,000 in all—130,000 in colleges and 250,000 in high schools. If my plan were followed, about 190,000 of these teachers would be thrown out of work. School teachers being for the most part people of good character and superior intellectual ability, I feel sure that the vast majority of them could make themselves useful almost anywhere in our society. But they would need time in which to find new fields suited to themselves and to acquire the necessary training for the jobs of their choice. To ensure that they were amply compensated for their sacrifice, I think the government should agree to pay their salaries for three full years after their dismissal, during which time they would be free to do whatever they pleased. This should be enough time for them to find new jobs and adjust to them, and I suspect that many of the teachers would end up contributing more to society than they do now. If the system of examinations mentioned earlier were put into effect, there would be many more people who studied while working and quite a few teachers might find work tutoring or holding classes for such people. In any event, I seriously doubt whether the ex-teachers, if given time to adjust, would end up without jobs. Many might well be happier.

In this connection, it seems to me that we are paying out so much money to build educational facilities that there is not enough left to pay our teachers adequately. I believe, therefore, that if my plan were followed, the salaries of the teachers remaining in the schools should be doubled. If this were done, the many teachers who now have to supplement their incomes with outside work would be free to devote themselves body and soul to the important work of education. The results, I think, would be something that could not be measured in terms of money.

In order to double the pay of teachers, pay three years' salary to ex-teachers and buy up land and facilities belonging to defunct private schools, the country would have to disburse trillions of yen. Even though in the long run this would be a good investment, the fact is that the government does not have that much money to invest in anything. The solution, I believe, would be a large flotation of low-interest national bonds, but I shall take this up in more detail later.

It is essential that the revolutionary plan I have proposed be carried out resolutely and thoroughly. Many might object to the plan at the outset, but if I myself were a college teacher or a high school teacher, I do not think I would oppose it. And the fact is that we must carry out some plan of this sort if our country is to survive.

Fees for hiring graduates

In the government universities, the average cost of putting one student through the normal four-year college course is said to be about ¥3,000,000 ($10,000), the amount of tuition paid by the student during this time being only ¥144,000 ($480). The cost per student varies, of course, with the university and with the course that the student is taking (the cost for science majors is considerably greater than that for liberal arts students), but for purposes of this discussion, we can take ¥3,000,000 as the figure. (This amount, it might be noted, would be much greater if the interest that might otherwise be received on school properties were figured in.)

It is a well-known fact that after graduation, students who have been educated at such great expense to the nation go to work, for the most part, either for the government—as bureaucrats or as teachers in government schools—or for big business. Only a small proportion seek employment in small enterprises or set out on their own.

If the graduate goes to work for the government, then the ¥3,000,000 that the government has spent on him may be considered as the fee that the government has paid to train a new employee. The situation is different, however, when graduates go to work for business concerns, and particularly when so many of them go into large business concerns. It is true, of course, that big businesses pay big taxes; but small businesses pay taxes at the same rate, and it is exceedingly unfair that the big corporations should receive most of the benefits from the taxes spent on the education of students, whereas small businesses are rarely able to hire them. Many medium and small businessmen complain about this, and rightly so.

It seems to me that the situation could be remedied by requiring all business concerns hiring graduates of government universities to pay an average of ¥3,000,000 to the government for the privilege of doing so. The actual amount could be fixed by law and adjusted in such a way as to take into account the varying costs of the individual student's training.

Similar fees would be paid to local governments that operate universities, on a scale corresponding to the amount actually spent on each student's education. Presumably, if the average fee for a graduate from a national university were ¥3,000,000, the fee for a graduate of a local university would be roughly the same. In the case of private universities, which are subsidized by the government, a fee of about one-third this amount, or ¥1,000,000, should be paid. I think the same idea might be extended to include graduates of high schools who go to work for private businesses.

Business circles as a whole would probably oppose such a system vigorously, for the total fee would amount to quite a lot in the case of companies that hire tens and hundreds of high school or college graduates each year. In my opinion, however, when a private business hires a graduate of a public school, it is acquiring a product made at public expense, and it is only proper that the public receive proper compensation.

If businessmen had to pay ¥3,000,000 each for graduates of government universities, they would be a great deal more careful than they are now about whom they hire and how they employ him. It would no longer be a case, as it is now, of grabbing up a certain number of college graduates each year just in case they turn out to be useful someday. Businessmen would want to make sure that they were getting their ¥3,000,000's worth, and in the long run increased selectivity would no doubt be profitable to their companies. It should also be easier for medium and small businesses to hire graduates of government colleges. Or at any rate, I think that if they remained unable to hire such graduates, they would at least not feel that it was because of systematic discrimination.

I believe this procedure would also cause students to take a closer look at themselves, for they would soon see that people are not going to pay ¥3,000,000 to hire just anybody. This knowledge would probably make most students study harder and try to develop their personalities to a point where someone would be willing to pay the necessary fee for them. As I have remarked several times before, there are all too many students who go to high school or college for no other reason than that this is the fashion of our times. The method I am proposing might well weed out quite a few of these and make it easier to reduce the number of colleges and high schools. Indeed, the idea of a fee for hiring graduates works in extremely well with the educational revolution that I have in mind. It would improve the quality of education, reduce waste, and have a favorable effect upon prices, as well.

Fewer schools and more education

Not long ago, I had an opportunity to talk with Minister of Education Nagai. During our meeting, he emphasized that "going to school and learning are two different things." I could not agree more.

The fundamental aim of education is to produce human beings who are sound of mind and body, and who possess the combination of knowledge, feeling, and determination needed to contribute to the general welfare. The system of education we have today, which lays greatest stress on the intellectual knowledge required to pass a series of entrance examinations leading from kindergarten through college, is fundamentally out of line with the basic purpose and should be corrected as quickly as possible.

It could be corrected in a number of ways, but I believe that if the revisions I have outlined for the school system were adopted, it would correct itself. My idea, basically, is that compulsory education should concern itself with making true human beings out of young people, and that advanced education should be broadened in such a way as to make it possible for people to acquire formal qualifications without attending institutions of higher learning. In this chapter, I have tried to show how this idea could best be carried out by simply reducing the number of high schools and colleges now in operation.

Price Stability and Large-scale Economic Development

An emergency price stabilization law

I have stressed several times that since the inflation confronting us is a product of wastefulness and inefficiency in our way of life, the basic solution will require a number of long-term revolutionary measures calculated to eliminate waste and raise efficiency. There remains, however, the question of what we should do *right now* to stop the rise of prices and keep it stopped. My answer is that we should devise an emergency price stabilization law that would freeze prices without violating the principles of a free economy.

The first provision of this law would be that as of January 1, 1975, all fees for public utilities under the jurisdiction of the national and local governments must for three years be held to a level no higher than on that date. It would be permissible to lower the fees, but not to raise them.

In the Tokugawa period (1603–1868), it was a common practice in times of famine and other emergencies for the lords of the various fiefs to dole out to the people rice from the fiefs' storehouses. If we were able to do that in the feudal period, it should be possible for our government now, in view of the current emergency, to give the people a break on public utilities. The principle is much the same.

The second provision would be that as of January 1, 1975, all prices, including those for raw materials, for consumer goods or for services of any sort, must for three years be kept below the level of that date. The law would also encourage businessmen to try to reduce prices below that level by allowing them to make a reasonable profit, in accordance with the principles of free enterprise and competition. It would be saying to the businessmen, in effect, "Make your legitimate profit, but do so while lowering prices."

The third provision would be that wages and similar compensation would be pegged at the level prevalent on January 1, 1975, with the exception that at the time of the annual spring wage increases, management and labor might, through free negotiations, agree upon a rise not in excess of five percent. This wage freeze would also continue for three years. Unfixed wages, such as those received by day laborers, would be decided upon by the Ministry of Labor, which in determining the amount would take into consideration the levels prevailing on January 1, 1975, and the level of wages among fixed-wage earners. Such wages would also be allowed to increase up to five percent per year.

The emergency price stabilization law might be administered by an appropriate branch of the government or by a special committee chosen by the government and confirmed by the Diet. Should the latter be the case, it should be stipulated that members of the committee must have had at least twenty years of successful business experience and be no older than sixty-five.

At present, economic activity is sluggish, and the normal procedure would be to give the economy a shot in the arm; but since that would no doubt cause prices to go up, the policy now in effect is one of holding back demand in general. If, however, there were a definite ceiling on prices, and if the laws of free competition were allowed to work, it would be possible for the economy to recover and economic activity to expand without the danger of further inflation. If, at the same time, the number of high schools and colleges were reduced by half, there would be no more labor problem. This in itself would enable us to proceed actively with what could be called cultural construction, such as the building of new houses, the construction of needed roads, and the beautification of our landscape. Such work is, after all, necessary for our future.

Imported goods

If the price freeze were carried out uniformly, a number

of problems would arise, and there would have to be a fourth provision in the law to take care of them.

One problem would result from price movements in other countries. As far as domestic goods are concerned, it would be possible, if we really put our minds to it, to hold the line on prices for three years, but, as can be seen from the case of oil alone, Japan has no control over the price of raw materials coming in from foreign countries. We should, I think, as a matter of principle, discuss this matter on a friendly basis with other countries and try to persuade them to sell us their commodities at the lowest possible prices; but there would certainly be instances in which the foreign countries could not avoid a price increase. The question is what we should do in instances of this type.

My answer is that the prices should be kept fixed within Japan anyway. The Japanese government would pay the increment in cost, or at least most of it (I believe that business should be made to absorb two percent of the increase, leaving the government to pay the other ninety-eight percent). In return, when products made from these materials are exported, at international prices, the exporters should reimburse the government for the amount it had put up at the time of importation. This rule would be applied not only to companies importing directly, but to companies making products for which twenty percent or more of the cost is spent on imported materials.

Theoretically, if the government paid for ninety-eight percent of the increase in cost for imported materials, Japanese exporters could reduce their export prices by a corresponding amount. This, however, would play havoc with the international market and would therefore meet with strong foreign opposition. The export prices should therefore be kept at the international level, and the difference between that and the domestic price be paid back to the government.

This would admittedly be a little tricky from the practical viewpoint, because even if the subsidy given by the Japanese government were reclaimed at the time of export, there would probably be those in foreign countries who would charge that the Japanese government was collaborating with Japanese manufacturers in undercutting international prices. This objection would have to be met by diplomatic means and by extensive public relations campaigns in other countries.

Another problem would arise in connection with foodstuffs. It is comparatively easy to fix the prices of industrial products, but in the case of food, prices may by affected by numerous factors beyond human control. Too little rainfall, for example, can lead to a shortage of vegetables, and a typhoon can easily reduce the supply of fish temporarily. Even a train accident or some other unforeseen breakdown in the ordinary distribution process can cause a sudden increase in costs. It would therefore be difficult, I suspect, to freeze the price of food as rigidly as in the case of manufactured goods. The price stabilization law, accordingly, would have to allow for a certain amount of flexibility in this area. To guard against excessive increases, the government would have to appoint supervisors to set a suitable level as the occasion demanded. In practice, the government's task in this connection could be delegated to unions of producers and dealers, who would be responsible for deciding upon their own rules as well as on a system of penalties for violators. I believe that the unions, if given this responsibility, would carry it out faithfully, though of course they would be subject to supervision by the government. The point would be to make it clear to the unions that though temporary price increases because of climate and other factors would be allowed, the overall level for the year would have to remain in line with prices prevailing within Japan in general.

If prices were fixed in this fashion for three years, there might very well be companies claiming that they could not meet the selling prices without going into the red. In cases of this sort, the procedure should be for such companies to apply to the government for relief, and for the government then to investigate their claims thoroughly. If the government should find that a company had made a sincere effort to keep its prices down, but was still unable to make ends meet, then the government would allow that company the subsidy needed to provide it with a minimal profit. An increase in prices, however, would not be tolerated.

Economic stabilization bonds

There next arises the question of where the government would obtain the funds needed to cover increased costs of imported goods or to subsidize companies unable to sell at the frozen prices. Where, again, would the government find funds needed to carry out the reform in the education system proposed in the last chapter?

Since, as I have said before, the government has no money tree, nor any means of supplying its needs on its own, the necessary funds would in the long run have to come from the people in the form of increased taxes or purchases of national bonds. In these difficult times, there is a serious danger that an increase in taxes would reduce the people's incentive to work. Indeed, I would be more inclined at the moment to favor a general tax reduction. The only remaining possibility is a bond flotation, which, if carried out at currently prevailing interest rates, would place an intolerable burden on the government's financial resources.

For this reason, I think there should be a fifth provision in the price stabilization law calling for the issue of economic stabilization bonds and making it compulsory for all companies and individuals to purchase them. These bonds, which would be perhaps the most important support for the price stabilization law, would bear an interest of only two percent. They would be nontransferable, and the stipulation would be that after five years the government would redeem them at the rate of twenty percent annually. At an interest rate of two percent, the interest that the government would pay on one hundred trillion yen would be only two trillion yen per annum, an amount that could be made up by reducing national expenditures by only ten percent. Such an amount is no cause for alarm, and the question is whether we can be decisive enough to carry out the measure and use it as a means for constructive reforms.

It is to be anticipated that no one will want to buy bonds at such a low rate of interest, but these economic stabilization bonds would in no sense be the same as ordinary bonds. They would be emergency bonds needed to curb inflation, to prevent Japan from collapsing, and to start a new program of economic development. It would therefore make sense, even at a time when companies and individuals alike are suffering from low revenues, to require everyone to purchase the bonds in accordance with his ability.

This is part of what I meant earlier when I said that everyone would have to bear his share of the pain resulting from the surgery our country needs. Nobody likes low-interest bonds, but they represent the only means of stopping inflation and carrying out an education reform. Without them, we shall continue to operate in the red until the country sinks. Therefore, I feel it is justifiable to compel a person with an income of one hundred million yen to buy, say, fifty million yen's worth of bonds, and a person with an income of ten thousand yen would have to buy a hundred yen's worth. This would be shedding a drop of blood for the nation, but by this means, it would be possible to put an end to inflation.

Cutting national expenditures by twenty percent

If the emergency price stabilization law were put into effect, then wages would increase somewhat over the next three years, but prices would stay the same. Actually, it is more likely that prices would come down, because the pressures of competition would force businesses to take a new look at themselves and to streamline their operations. We would have more efficient management and production, and there would be greater incentive to increase productivity by means of new methods and creative ideas. Personnel expenses would be limited to an increase of five percent annually, and other costs, including those for materials, would stay the same. In such an atmosphere, it is most likely that efficiency would go up and prices would come down in a general campaign to outdo the competition.

The question is whether during those three years we would have the ability to work and cooperate with each other to hold down prices and carry out needed social reforms. It is one thing to outline methods, but it is quite another thing to carry out a revolutionary program of this sort over a period of three years. If the reforms were not successful, then even after keeping prices frozen for three years, we would still find ourselves faced with the same inflationary conditions as before. In the last few years, a number of countries have attempted to freeze prices and wages for a period of time, but though this method has yielded temporary results, the lifting of the freeze has been followed by a round of huge price increases. The difficulty, I think, has been that the measures needed to eradicate inflationary pressures were not carried out during the period in which prices were frozen.

To avoid simply repeating the experience of foreign countries, Japan will need to carry out many reforms during the time of her price freeze. The first is a drastic reduction in national and public expenditures, which will have to be accomplished by means of a thorough rationalization in the various branches of the national government as well as in the local governments. Personally, I think the goal should be a twenty percent reduction in government expenditures, and I think it should be accompanied by an increase, rather than a decrease, in public services. In short, what the government is now doing for one trillion yen should be done for eight hundred billion yen; what is being done by ten people should be done by eight people; and efficiency should be increased in the process. Certain attempts have been made at rationalization in the past, but what I have in mind is a more thoroughgoing and resolute housecleaning than we have ever seen. We must start not from the idea that we will do this if we can, but from the idea that we will do it, period. Then we must take the necessary steps, which may entail reducing personnel, introducing new machinery, and simplifying both organization and procedures. A reduction of twenty percent is certainly drastic, but I do not think it is impossible.

A comparison between now and forty years ago, or 1935, shows that the beginning salary of Japanese college graduates has increased by thirteen hundred times, and the general price level by a thousand times, but the level of government expenditures has increased by more than 13,000 times. Since we have better transportation and communication now, not to speak of other improvements, one would think that government would be more efficient than before; but in fact we do not get 13,000 times as much or even thirteen times as much from the government as we got in 1935.

(In this connection, I find myself troubled by doubts concerning the effect of computers on American society. Theoretically, the use of computers in government and business should lead to greater efficiency and bring about a host of benefits, but in the United States, where these machines have been used very extensively for fifteen years, there seem to be more political and social difficulties than ever. Prices have gone up tremendously, and the people show signs of unrest and discontent. Computers appear to have added to the nation's troubles instead of reducing them, and I wonder why this is.)

A reduction of twenty percent in government expenses would naturally lead to a decrease in prices in general. It would also make possible a reduction in taxes and a corresponding increase in real wages. The benefits, therefore, would be twofold.

Such a rationalization, like the educational reform I have proposed, would lead to a temporary displacement of personnel. This is not intrinsically a serious problem, since business is capable in the long run of absorbing the people thrown out of work. At the same time, personnel released should be kept on the government payroll at their current wages until they have had time to find suitable employment. As in the case of teachers displaced by the educational reform, this period might be set at a maximum of three years, and the cost to the government would be defrayed with funds made available by the economic stabilization bonds.

Eliminating deficit management in public enterprises

I think it is also necessary to carry out a thorough restructuring of public enterprises, many of which are now causing a great financial drain on national and local governments. Drastic measures are needed to make it possible for these enterprises to operate in the black. To this end, I think the government should establish a committee for the improvement of management in public enterprises, composed of members selected by the government and confirmed by the National Diet. The membership should be small and should include, for the most part, men under sixty-five with twenty years or more of successful business experience. There should be a sprinkling of scholars, but businessmen should form the majority. The committee should start with those enterprises that are in the worst financial condition and work up to those that are operating fairly smoothly, devising plans whereby management could be improved. In principle, the committee's findings would be in the nature of advice, but if the managers of public enterprises should prove unable or unwilling after two or three warnings to carry out the committee's advice, the committee should have the power to change managers. It should also be within the committee's authority to divest the government of any enterprise that in its opinion would better be left in private hands.

I feel certain that the presence of such a committee would lead to improved management and increased productivity in public enterprises, and that the result would be lower prices for government services. A number of enterprises would doubtless begin to show a profit, in which case they should be required to pay taxes on it. In other words, they would be paying taxes instead of using them up, and the benefit to the people would be enormous. The effect on prices in general would also be salutary.

In my opinion, there is a need within the framework of a free economy not only for government enterprises to improve their performance, but for various business concerns and various fields of business to review their economic activities with an eye to increasing efficiency. Indeed, this could be said of the economy as a whole. If, with prices frozen, it is possible for companies to take all the profits they can make, then they will be encouraged to find new and original means of rationalizing their operations, increasing their productivity, and lowering their costs. This activity might well be reflected in the lives of individuals as well, for certainly many of them would become more conscious of the need for efficiency in their daily activities.

If we all undertake to attack the problems of inefficiency and waste, then we will find that after three years prices will have been genuinely stabilized, and controls are no longer necessary. We will also find that our income is greater. Of course, if the reforms that I am urging are actually carried out, some people and some businesses will doubtless feel an adverse effect for a time. For example, businesses that supply equipment to schools would suffer a reduction in sales if the number of schools were cut in half. But such ill effects would be of limited scope and duration, and the total effect on the economy of the nation would be a great increase in business activity as well as in the general prosperity.

And there would be a corresponding increase in demand for new products and new services.

If we are to arrive at this new prosperity, however, we must work night and day on the stabilization of prices. We should go full speed ahead without bothering too much about niceties, and if problems arise, solve them as the situation demands. During these three years, we should not adopt the comfortable view that there are 365 days in a year, but rather work ourselves up to the pitch of trying to do in thirty days what we would normally do in 365.

Making a paradise of Japan

In my view, the emergency price stabilization law would not be a negative measure, but would become a positive incentive toward increased economic activity throughout the nation. We would not merely be limiting prices, but would be offering businesses, under a system of free enterprise, the opportunity to increase their profits by increasing their efficiency. There are many things that need to be done in Japan today to improve the lives of the people and increase the benefits they enjoy. We need, for example, greater protection for our natural environment; we need better sewage systems, better housing, and improved social facilities. In these areas, we still lag far behind the advanced countries of the West, and there is a need for both the government and private enterprise to attack these areas quickly and in a constructive fashion.

At present, however, much of the work that needs to be done to improve our national life is held up because of the rising cost of construction materials and labor. If prices were stabilized, and if at the same time capital were made available through the economic stabilization bonds, it would be possible to undertake an enormous amount of public construction. The flotation of the economic stabilization bonds, then, would not only achieve the purpose of stopping inflation, but would also make possible much new economic activity of a truly significant nature.

Japan is by no means a large country, and yet seventy percent of its total area consists of forest-covered mountains. There are many locations where human beings have barely set foot. It seems to me important for Japan's future to develop these areas and make good use of all the territory we have. By development, I do not, of course, mean destroying our natural assets. The purpose would be to make the most of these, while at the same time increasing their value to us.

Switzerland, which is known for its beautiful scenery, attracts tourists from all over the world, but the mountains and lakes of Switzerland, for all their magnificence, cannot compare in number and variety with those of Japan—where there are not only mountains and lakes, but rivers, the ocean, and immensely varied combinations of these natural elements. In addition to this, Japan has a moderate climate, in which each of the four seasons presents its own beauties. If we succeeded in making the scenery of Japan available in all its infinite variety, surely the country would become a veritable wonderland for tourists. We owe it not only to ourselves, but to the other people of the world to do so. When you stop to consider it, perhaps the scenic loveliness of our islands is the most valuable natural resource of all, and it is one which, unlike iron ore or petroleum, need not be used up. Far from depleting this resource, we could, if we went about it the right way, enhance its value tremendously.

I think it would be most appropriate and significant for the Japanese nation to make of itself a mecca for those who love to visit beautiful places, for if Japan were to become a paradise, there would be all the less danger of its becoming involved in war. This may sound farfetched, but I do not think it really is. If Japan develops its natural scenery in the right way, it might well come to be regarded as a place that should not be subject to warfare under any circumstances. Such things are possible: even Hitler refrained from bombing the beautiful city of Paris, and although most Japanese cities suffered air raids, Kyoto and Nara, the two great cultural centers of the past, were spared. So long as Japan avoids war, then, it seems unlikely that other countries would make a target of a much more beautiful Japan.

To arrive at this state, however, it is not enough

simply to beautify our terrain. We must also be a country with attitudes and spiritual values worthy of a physical paradise. In the material sense, we must have towns with beautiful streets, excellent facilities, and splendid environmental surroundings. Our sewage system should be better than that of Paris, and our houses better and more comfortable than those of Europe and America. More than that, however, we must cultivate our minds and hearts. We must be the best-mannered people in the world, and we must develop a way of life that will be an inspiration to those who visit our country.

To build a country of this sort, to enhance its natural scenery, to create beautiful cities with splendid facilities and environments—all this would be the greatest national enterprise we have ever undertaken, and would, of course, require an enormous amount of capital. This money, too, could be raised through flotations of economic stabilization bonds, though in this case we are talking not of a three-year campaign, but of programs that would require twenty-five years or more.

How much money would be needed? I have not considered the matter in detail, but I would suppose the program I have in mind would cost about a hundred trillion yen. By a very rough calculation, if five hundred thousand persons per day were employed in this project for twenty-five years, personnel expenses would run to about twenty-five trillion, leaving seventy-five trillion for construction materials and the like. The bonds covering this could be issued a trillion yen at a time over the twenty-five years, with several flotations in a single year so that the maximum outstanding amount would be one hundred trillion yen. This should be enough to cover the outlay while at the same time keeping prices down and providing economic stability. Although I say "enough," however, this beautification program would never be completed, for in the course of carrying it out, we would discover new projects that we wanted to undertake. Still, we should make a basic plan for twenty-five years and at the end of that time follow it with another similar plan.

Let me stress once again that I do not conceive of the economic stabilization bonds merely as a means of holding down inflation and cooling off the economy. They would also have the more positive purpose of developing our natural landscape, nurturing our national spirit, providing us with a magnificent environment, and ultimately making Japan as a nation into an international paradise. We might even call them "bonds for natural beauty," or "bonds for ideal development."

Reservoir management

We long ago learned not to let the water in rivers simply flow unhindered into the sea, but rather to dam it up and release it as necessary to make the most effective use of it, whether for irrigation, for hydroelectric power, or for some other purpose. It is my strong belief that businesses should be managed like reservoirs and that the principle of the dam should be applied to the management of our government and to our own individual lives as well. For if there is always a reservoir of strength, it becomes possible for us to have stability in our personal lives, stability in business, and stability in the management of national affairs.

I think of the economic stabilization bonds as a great dam creating a reservoir from the little streams that flow in from each and every one of the people. The reservoir thus created can be used for positive, constructive national projects and large-scale reforms, while at the same time serving to prevent inflation and stabilize prices—in short, it would be an invaluable source of strength.

Critics might suggest that the construction program I have in mind would cause increased consumption, together with large growth in related industries, and would therefore lead to further inflation. My belief, however, is that the experience we would gain from three years of frozen prices would enable us to prevent such an outcome. Moreover, if the threat of inflation were to arise once again, the process outlined for bringing it under control could simply be repeated, without bringing a halt to progressive economic activity. In fact, I think that if we were to employ this basic mode of operation for the next fifteen years, responding with additional revolutionary programs whenever necessary, Japan would become the most nearly ideal nation in the world.

It may be further objected that at times like these, it would be a great burden on the people to have to purchase low-interest bonds. I am aware of this, but I believe that there is no other way out of our present threatening circumstances. More than anything else, we need the determination to save ourselves.

THE AUTHOR: Born in 1894 in Wakayama, Matsushita went to work at an early age. Concluding that good-quality electrical wiring apparatus would soon be in great demand, in 1918, together with his wife and brother-in-law, he founded a pioneering electric house-wares works. At first designing and marketing plugs, Matsushita expanded his company and it was incorporated in 1935 as Matsushita Electric Industrial Co., Ltd. Matsushita served as president, chairman, and, since his retirement in 1973, as adviser to the company whose diverse products are best known abroad by the brand names of "National," "Panasonic" and "Technics."

Matsushita has contributed widely to contemporary life in Japan, as a director of various industries, adviser to economic and business associations, and founder of the PHP Institute for social research. He has received honorary degrees from three universities and has repeatedly been decorated by the government. His many books have found a wide reading public.